Thank you for having me a
support through my travel.
While Ayers Rock isn't featured, there is
wonderful scenery that I hope will bring
back memories of your Canadian / Singapore/
Aussie friend.

Adele

SURFING THE MENU

SURFING THE MENU

Two chefs, one journey: a fresh-food adventure

Ben O'Donoghue AND Curtis Stone

Photographs by Ben Dearnley, Craig Kinder and Ewan Robinson

ABC
Books

FOR CAROLYN FOULNER

The publishers would like to thank the following organisations for kindly supplying homewares and props for use during food photography: All Hand Made, Anibou, Arte Flowers Sydney, Atmosphere, Bison Homewares, Cambodia House, Chee Soon & Fitzgerald, Country Road, The Essential Ingredient, Michael Greene Antiques, Mrs Red & Son, Orrefors Kosta Boda, Orson & Blake, Papaya, Planet Furniture, Russian Empire Trading Company, and Spence & Lyda.

Published by ABC Books for the
AUSTRALIAN BROADCASTING CORPORATION
GPO Box 9994 Sydney NSW 2001

First published February 2004

National Library of Australia
Cataloguing-in-Publication entry
    O' Donoghue, Ben.
    Surfing the Menu : two chefs, one journey : a fresh food adventure

    Includes index.
    ISBN 0 7333 1301 9.

    1. Cookery, Australian. 2. Australians - Food. 3. Surfing
    - Australia. I. Dearnley, Ben. II. Stone, Curtis. III.
    Kinder, Craig. IV Robinson, Ewan. V. Australian
    Broadcasting Corporation. VI. Title.

641.5994

Designed by Nada Backovic
Photography by Ben Dearnley (food photography), Craig Kinder (Margaret River,
New Norcia, Abrolhos Islands and Broome) and Ewan Robinson (Tasmania, Bellarine Peninsula,
Hunter Valley and Byron Bay)
Food styling by Kristen Anderson
Home economists Rebecca Truda and Jo Glynn
Maps by Geoff Morrison
Set in Univers 10/16pt
Colour reproduction by PageSet, Victoria
Printed and bound in Singapore by Tien Wah Press

5 4 3 2 1

Contents

Acknowledgements

Curtis Stone

Before I sit back and enjoy this book, I need to thank a few special people who have helped me to achieve it. When I was first asked to film a TV series with someone I didn't know particularly well and who had a different style of cooking to me, I naturally had some reservations. What was to unfold was a great friendship starting with a big night out with Ben and his mates when we first landed in Perth. By the end of the series and the book, I feel like he is not only my partner in crime but someone I can cook with, learn from and teach, not to mention sit up with until 7 am over a few bottles of vino talking about food for hours on end. So, Bender, thanks for everything.

Occasionally I feel privileged to be given all the amazing opportunities that I have had. Then I get a little arrogant about my life and remember the seventeen-hour days and the six-day weeks that I put in at my first kitchen in London. I don't think I could have learnt the value of hard work from a more qualified person than Marco Pierre White and his business partner, Jimmy La Houd.

An important side to running a restaurant like Quo Vadis is the trust you need to have in the people who work alongside you for sixteen hours a day. Without their dedication and hard work it would not be possible. Whether it is my first sous chef, Chris Hayworth, who is now the executive chef at La Rascasse in London or my second sous chef, Brendon Collins, who is now the head chef at Melisse on Venice Beach in Los Angeles or the loyal Graham Towner, who is now working with me on the new concept for a restaurant in Chelsea, London; their support has definitely helped me achieve all I have to this day.

My early inspiration came from dear Lozza, my mum; her love of good natural food will never leave me. Speaking of family I would also like to thank my father, Mr Finance, for putting a decent business head on my shoulders — this is an integral part of running any business. I come from a small family with only one brother, older than me and a bit of a tough lad. When we were younger, he gave me a few clips behind the ears, which probably gave me the strength that I have now. He is a successful businessman whom I have learnt from and for whom I have an enormous amount of respect.

One of the first chefs I worked for was Enifred Barth at the Savoy Hotel in Melbourne. He taught met he importance of tradition in food; he was very classically trained and he passed that on to me. He is now passing on some of his knowledge, teaching at Melbourne's leading catering college, among other things, and remains a dear friend of mine.

Working on 'Surfing the Menu' has been a lovely break for me from a hectic kitchen. It has given me the opportunity to broaden my knowledge and appreciation of fresh ingredients at a grass-root level — which has further inspired me in the kitchen.

I would like to thank the producer and scriptwriter — Marian and Alun Bartsch — two very driven people who brought 'Surfing the Menu' to life. Furthermore, Marian put together a crew who were more professional than I thought possible, and included two brilliant stills photographers — Ewan Robinson and Craig Kinder — one of whom also had the ability to teach me to surf. Cheers Craig!

I hope you all enjoy the book as much as I have enjoyed putting it together. It would not have been possible without the creativity of a dedicated editor (Susan Morris-Yates), stylist (Kristen Anderson), photographer (Ben Dearnley) and home economists (Rebecca Truda and Jo Glynn).

Last but by no means least, I would like to thank my best mate, Chris Sheldon, who is not only the best bartender in London, but who has the ability no matter how hectic my life gets to keep a smile on my face.

Ben O'Donoghue

There are so many people I need to thank who were involved in making the TV program and the book, but more than anything else I need to say a big 'I love you' and thanks for putting up with me to my gorgeous partner, De-Arne, who single-handedly looked after our baby daughter, Ruby, for two months while I was off filming this project. You're amazing and I love you dearly.

I would also like to thank my family in Australia for always being my biggest supporters: my mum and dad; grandma; my brother Daniel and his wife Tania, and my nephew Benjie; also my new family, Peter, Jewels, Neil and Kate, for making me feel part of the family.

Thank you, Marian, for your unlimited energy and pure determination to get this all off the ground, and for having faith in Stoney and me. Also, Martine, thank you for putting up with Marian, Stoney and me (ha ha!). Thanks to the best film crew I've had the pleasure of working with (Geoff, Uli, Bubbli aka Paul, Laurie, Kelvin); to Ewan and Craig for taking the best goddamn pictures of Australia I have ever seen (mind you, you just have to point a camera in Australia and it looks great); to Kerrie for getting us all out of bed; and to Ursula for making miracles happen — you're a gem. And how can I forget Alun: you're a legend. Love those hats, mate!

To you all, four-twenty forever!

To Susan Morris-Yates, thanks a million for putting together a wonderful book over 30,000 kilometres away; for the many large emails too big for my hot mail account to handle, and for stretching deadlines to accommodate difficult chefs. To Ben and Kristen and Bec, thanks for all the hard work shooting the food within such a tight schedule and for putting up with the stress.

A big thank you to all the characters who appeared in the series. Herb and Gruff, thanks for the Tassie experience, and thanks to everyone else that made us so welcome. To Lozza and Golly: you're fantastic and Ruby looks beautiful in the cardie you knitted.

And finally, a big thanks to Curtis Stone for making me look good in water and bad on land!

Love to everyone I may have forgotten.

Bender

Ben O'Donoghue

BEN O'DONOGHUE

I was five when my family moved from England to Australia (for free, it now costs heaps!). My parents travelled heaps when I was young so I never saw much of England. I've always felt and sounded Australian, although I'm glad that I have a British passport, I doubt if my life would have turned out the way it has otherwise.

We moved to a town called Port Hedland in the north-west of Western Australia, one of the best places where a kid could grow up. I suppose this is where I started to cook; We'd build fires on the beach, catch fish and cook them on corrugated iron sheets, ripped off roofs in cyclones, and bake potatoes in the coals.

When I was ten, my family moved south to Perth, where my brother and I went to school. On finishing, I got a job on Rottnest Island for the summer. I loved it so much (sun, surf, girls, etc.) that I got a job in the kitchen of the Rottnest Restaurant as a kitchen hand. This was the perfect job scenario, that is, surf-work-pub. There was great camaraderie among the chefs and I found I had a talent in the cooking department. I thought I should get an apprenticeship. A couple of interviews later, I was working in a busy Nedlands fish restaurant called Jojo's doing about eighty hours a week (the honeymoon was over) and loving it.

After qualifying as a chef, I was promoted to Sous Chef at Jessica's Seafood Restaurant in Perth, but felt the need to spread my wings, so I headed east to Sydney. I managed to secure a position as a Chef de Partie at a new restaurant called Goodfella's, in the inner west suburb of Newtown. I was shortly promoted to Sous Chef. In 1993, the restaurant was awarded the Best New Restaurant Award by *The Sydney Morning Herald Good Food Guide,* and the following year two chef's hats.

Jobs and chefs come and go, and I went travelling, chasing the dream of the perfect wave. I found myself on the frost-bitten earth of old Blighty in the middle of May 1996 on my twenty-sixth birthday. I promptly bought a food guide, looked up the best restaurants in town and started looking for work. I didn't have to look for long — the second place I went to was The River Café where I somehow managed to secure a job. The River Café was the most inspirational place I've ever had the pleasure to work. The quality of chefs and the inspirational genius of Rose Gray and Ruthie Rodgers provided a highly motivated environment in which to work. Their ideas, philosophy and approach to Italian food provided the backbone of my own style of cooking.

At this time I met Jamie Oliver (yes, The Naked Chef) who had started just a few days earlier. Who was to know that Jamie's life would change so dramatically and that mine would run a similar course? During the whole Naked Chef thing, Jamie turned to his friends; to appear on *The Naked Chef* (I was on the show three times and had one episode dedicated to my birthday) and to help out with the food styling for his first and second cookbooks as well as a publicity tour to Australia and New Zealand (on this tour I met my girlfriend and mother of my beautiful baby girl, Ruby. Thanks mate!).

After all this I made a few connections of my own, and scored an agent — thinking that a little bit of extra work and pocket money would be great from doing demos and small-bit TV appearances. The next thing, Martine, my agent is saying 'Do you want to present a show in Morocco for American TV?' I'm like, Yeah, love to!

One thing led to another and I got a call to do a screen test for a new show on the BBC. I didn't think I'd get the job, especially after saying that my favourite food to cook was 'hash cookies', but they liked my style and my food and the rest is history. *The Best* came along with an accompanying book for the series in April 2002 on BBC2.

To think that I was doing nothing but TV work at the time would be far from reality. I had been approached by the management of the Hyatt Carlton Tower hotel in London to be Head Chef of Monte's, a restaurant, bar and night club in the fashionable shopping area of Knightsbridge. This was a fantastic opportunity to define and refine my style and philosophy on food: approachable, relaxed, hardworking with a good sense of humour and time for play!

And now that the challenges of making 'Surfing the Menu' are over, I'm looking forward to my next great adventure: taking control of the kitchen of one of the finest dining rooms in Great Britain — The Atlantic Bar and Grill.

Cooking for me is a passion and a reflex, it's something I've done since childhood and it never ceases to give pleasure or stimulate my imagination. I believe unequivocally that food should be simple and distinctive, technically and culturally correct. To say we eat with our eyes is rubbish: the senses of taste, smell and touch are far more important to me. Presentation should be secondary, but not discounted, and natural forms adhered to as much as possible. Use the best available seasonal produce, selecting from producers or suppliers with equal levels of integrity and passion as you have towards what you cook and eat.

Cooking for me is 50 per cent confidence, 40 per cent passion and 10 per cent technique and skill. Be brave and eat anything because experience is everything.

Curtis Stone

CURTIS STONE

Throughout my youth I had a few dreams. As a bit of a rebel, the Sex Pistols first inspired me to become a punk rocker. As I grew out of this, my next goal was to be up there with the best Aussie Rules footballers. Even though I had the mohawk haircut and Doc Martens, and played Aussie Rules at a good level, neither of them cut the mustard.

I have always loved eating — so much so that I consider myself greedy. I remember as a child my Mum (Lozza) baking her famous Anzac biscuits. I would watch her every move, dipping my finger into the dough at any given opportunity and waiting anxiously to get my hands on the wooden spoon while the biscuits went into the oven. The smell was fantastic, I would watch them bake, anticipating their taste. Dear Lozza still sends me a batch in London from time to time.

Once it was time to get out and do some work experience I got my first real taste of how a professional kitchen worked. It was complete madness: extreme heat, long hours, sharp objects, crazy people, blood, sweat and tears. I was excited by it and am sure I always will be. That was it, there were no more decisions to make. I did my apprenticeship at TAFE and began cooking at the Savoy Hotel in Melbourne; I spent the next five years or so working in some of Melbourne's best kitchens.

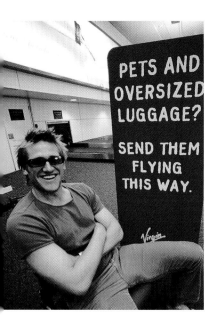

But then I felt the time had come to leave Melbourne to go in search of some new challenges, so I set off to Europe with my best mate, Tomaso. Our first port of call was Calabria, Tomaso's hometown in the south of Italy. We stayed on the family farm, which was a hive of activity. Each day three generations of women would spend the entire morning preparing the family lunch: making fresh pasta and collecting fruit and vegetables grown on the farm. The men of the family took great pride in showing me the pig, which they were fattening up to make into salamis and the home-grown grapes, which were turned into the family wine. Their entire life revolved around their lunch, and what a lunch it was. I could talk about that summer for weeks. It consisted of good food, learning the secrets of pasta dough, home baked breads, good wine, and the odd wild party. I think the main lesson I learnt about eating and cooking in Italy was to have respect for your raw ingredients.

My next port of call was London. In 1997 I began to work in Marco Pierre White's kitchen. Marco was Britain's most celebrated chef, the youngest chef in the world to win three Michelin stars. His reputation is deserved. He is as crazy as he is talented. Here I learnt about refined French cuisine. I started working with Spencer Patrick at the Grill Room (Café Royal), which was extremely formal. After twelve months, Marco opened a restaurant named Mirabelle, currently one of London's most famous eateries, and I was made Sous Chef there the year we won our first Michelin star. Only one year later, Marco appointed me Head Chef of another of his restaurants in London, Quo Vadis. By this time, Marco was out of the kitchen, which allowed me the freedom to incorporate more Italian influences in the food. The following year we were one of only four Italian restaurants to receive three rosette awards, and the restaurant has retained them to this day.

I loved my time at Quo Vadis, and if you ever get the chance, do eat there. I believe that good food can be as simple as using the best ingredients. I have a guy that brings me the best mozzarella from Naples every Tuesday. All I have to do is take a nice ripe tomato, chop it up, combine it with some fresh basil, salt and pepper, a drizzle of extra virgin olive oil and put the mozzarella on top for the perfect mozzarella and tomato salad. It couldn't be simpler or more delicious.

My passion for great food has now been extended further: working with great ingredients, well produced and at their best, has given me inspiration for a new style of restaurant. I am currently working with one of the world's leading restaurateurs, Sir Terence Conran, on an exciting new concept for London, based on ingredients, produce and respect for food.

I have eaten a lot of beautifully prepared food in my life, but one of my fondest memories is when my Dad took us to Apollo Bay in southern Victoria for a summer holiday when I was about seventeen. We were sitting on a balcony overlooking the beach with a bag of prawns, half a lemon and an ice cold Crown Lager. He said to me, 'I wonder what the poor people are doing today?'. We were not a wealthy family but I did feel like the king of the world.

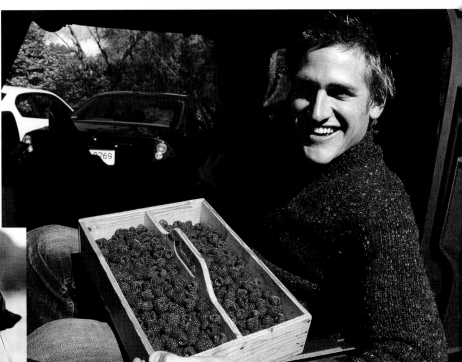

Curtis: Bender and I first met when we both appeared on a BBC show
called 'Saturday Kitchen'.

Ben: Yeah, and I had a bender of a hangover.

Curtis: Mate, you were no orphan, that day.

Ben: So, anyway, even though we were a little worse for wear, we had
fun together that day with the host, Gregg Wallace …

Curtis: And when Bender chose as his recipe presentation to do his
hangover cure, I knew we were going to be good mates.

Ben: Our lives working in London can sometimes be so rush, rush,
rush that sometimes I felt that I didn't have time to think.

Curtis: And in our business, that's dangerous — as new ideas, which are
the lifeblood of great menus, usually come from new experiences,
new attitudes and new people.

Ben: And every day, travelling on the same tube and the same bus can
sometimes give you tunnel vision, no pun intended.

Curtis: What I immediately found after I met Bender was that even though
so much of what we do, where we're from and what we've learnt
in our trade was so different, there was so much that we had in
common.

the beginning ...

Ben: For instance, I grew up on the west coast of Australia in Perth, starting out as a trainee school teacher. I took a part-time job in a kitchen on Rottnest Island (a holiday island just twelve kilometres off the coast) where I quickly figured out that if I could work in a restaurant and surf for the rest of the day, this would be as close to heaven as life could get ... especially if you added in girls. (Well, I was young and impressionable at that stage ...)

Curtis: Whereas, I started out doing a Bachelor of Business at university before it became clear to me that my passion was for the hot stoves of the kitchen, rather than the heat of the stock market ...

Ben: My cooking style has its roots in the Italian style.

Curtis: And mine is from a classic French perspective.

Ben: In other words, I'm a robust cook who gets into it — right up to my armpits and sometimes further ...

Curtis: And I'm a little more precise with my ingredients and my methods, shall we say.

Ben: But, the one big thing we found that we had in common when we met on that set of 'Saturday Kitchen' one cold, grey, London winter's day, was that we both really needed and craved an injection of what had got us passionate about cooking in the first place. So why not go back to our roots to reconnect with the motivations of our passion ...

Curtis: … And to look for inspiration in so many of the new things that had been happening back on the other side of the world, back home in Australia.

    Ben: And to fit in a surf. And girls … for Curtis, that is. I've got two beautiful girls in my life already.

Curtis: And because culinarily (is that a word?) Australia is changing at such a rapid rate … reinventing the classics and creating exciting, new genres.

    Ben: And don't forget a surf.

Curtis: The clean and green environment has meant so many opportunities …

    Ben: And to have a surf.

Curtis: So that's why we decided to go, together.

    Ben: And to have a surf.

Curtis: So there you have it. It's all about the food and the produce.

    Ben: And the surf.

Curtis: Oh yeah, and the surf … which, I must confess right up front, I'm actually not all that good at … but I'm happy to have a crack.

    Ben: 'It's only practice, my son,' I said. That was all that was holding us back.

Curtis: And the fact that, at that stage, you hadn't told your partner, Dee, just yet.

Ben: A minor technicality, but as you now know, Dee being the good Aussie sort she is, gave her blessing.

Curtis: Is that how it happened?

Ben: OK, there were some discussions and conditions, but they were minor.

Curtis: Then you found out that Dee was pregnant with your first child!

Ben: Yeah, that was a bit of a shock. But being the good sort I previously mentioned, Dee insisted that we go, just as long as we ended up in Byron Bay, where her dad and brother and sisters live, for a party for the brand new bubby.

Curtis: What an excellent woman. Does she have a single sister, mate?

Ben: So, that's how it all started. And in this book you can get a chance for yourself to see just how it all ended up: where we went and some of the great people we met, the fabulous produce we found and what inspired us to create a whole bunch of exciting new recipes.

Curtis: Plus, I'd like you to look closely at the surfing photos that have been carefully edited to make it look as though I was moderately successful in getting up and staying up.

Ben: You did all right, mate, you did OK.

Curtis: Well, there's always next time …

ABOUT THE TRIP

Abrolhos Islands

BEN: Since I was a kid I'd wanted to go to the Abrolhos, a rolling three-hours boat ride off the coast of Geraldton in Western Australia. The 122 islands are clustered in three main groups off the mid-west coast. There are only a handful of places in the world that can be compared to the Abrolhos and, in many ways, even they can't be compared because this is a unique environment with some of the best coral reefs in the world. It's the home of the rock lobster industry in the west and to say that I love eating those little critters would be an understatement. The Abrolhos with their unbelievable pristine environment (think Great Barrier Reef, then add the colours of opal for the water) are also on the way out to deep water yellow and blue fin tuna fishing. These days they're also the home of a fledgling pearling industry. It's an amazing place and the fishermen are only able to live on the islands during the lobster fishing season for a couple of months at a time in fairly basic shacks that they and their families call home. We had even thought to fit in a surf out there, too, but on the day Captain Murray took us out to the break, three gigantic tiger sharks slid under the boat when we'd stopped. So, Curtis and I decided that going back to camp and ending the day with a beer was a better idea than ending up with the words 'shark bait' on our tombstones.

Broome

CURTIS: Even in Melbourne we'd heard about Broome up north in the Kimberley region of Western Australia. Up here it's not summer and winter, it's wet season and dry season with, as we found, some Broome-only seasons too. Plenty of rain, loads of sunshine and rich red soils guarantee that you can grow pretty much anything you want up here, where life seems as close to ideal as it can get. Catch fabulous fish off the beach or delicious mud cabs in the mangroves near town for dinner. Another great thing is the truly remarkable mixture of cultures that make up Broome, most of its inhabitants having originally being attracted here by the pearling industry that survives and thrives today. So, mix all of them together: the unbelievable environment, the delicious produce plus a group of people descendent from Malays, Japanese, South Sea Islanders, Europeans and Australian Aborigines and you've got a recipe for a remarkable and memorable visit.

Hunter Valley

CURTIS: I love great wine, and when you combine it with great food, I'm in heaven. So an opportunity to put the two together again on this trip (Margaret River, New Norcia, Tasmania and the Hunter Valley) was too good an opportunity to pass up. The Hunter Valley is about a two-hour drive north of Sydney and extends way up into the Barrington Tops. The region is lush and green and the rich volcanic soils and the regular rainfall have ensured that parts of it look more like Wales than the classic image of Australia. There are great vineyards there and so, purely in the interests of research, we took the opportunity to sample as many of them as we could. We met some great and passionate characters and we even did some horse riding while helping the stockmen round up the herd on a cattle station in the Barrington Tops. Thankfully, I am to horse riding what Bender is to surfing, so this was my turn to shine. Hi-ho Silver, away!

New Norcia

CURTIS: I had read about a Spanish monastery town, just 132 kilometres north of Perth in Western Australia, called New Norcia. Founded by Dom Salvado in 1846, New Norcia is today home for sixteen Benedictine monks. The architecture, with its strong Spanish flavour, dominates the Australian bush setting and the buildings are classsified by the National Trust. I was interested to see it for myself because of the Mediterranean influence (even to this day they produce the three Mediterranean staples of bread, wine and olives, and they still observe an afternoon siesta). Very civilised, I think. Ben told me he had played Aussie Rules footy there when he was a schoolkid, so that settled it, we had to check it out. Plus we were a hundred ks from the ocean, so there was no chance for Ben to show me up again in the surf. New Norcia is in the middle of what the West Australians call the 'wheat belt' — kilometre after kilometre of rolling pasture and wheat plains with sheep and cattle everywhere, and quite a few surprises, too.

Margaret River

BEN: When I was growing up in Perth, we'd often come to Margaret River to surf, party and play up. It's only a three-and-a-half-hour drive south from Perth to some of Western Australia's best beaches. Since I've been away the whole region has become a gourmet's delight with world-class produce: including game, seafood, vegetables and fruit, not to mention wine. A buddy of mine, Aaron Carr, who I did my apprenticeship with, is now head chef at Vasse Felix — so that means surf-time and, for old time's sake, party-time too. The region is bound on three sides by ocean, so the climate is mild. In between the towering forests, beautiful lush, green farmlands grow fabulous produce. With over sixty wineries in the region, it's not hard to get a drink either.

Tasmania

BEN: Ah, beautiful Tassie. What can I tell you about it that you don't already know? It's an island off the south-eastern tip of Australia. It looks more like Europe than Australia with its lush farmland, pure freshwater streams and spectacular mountains. They make some great beer there, the wines are pretty good and everything else is special, too. This was not my first trip there, I'd visited and stayed with Gruff and Sandra a number of times before, as they were the parents of a mate I shared a house with for a few years in Sydney. So I was pretty familiar with the place and I thought it appropriate that I show Curtis around. I have surfed there in the past, but because it was a fair old drive from where we were staying in beautiful Strahan, we didn't get the boards off the roof. Hope we didn't look like poseurs driving around …

Bellarine Peninsula

CURTIS: The Bellarine Peninsula, just 24 kilometres south of Geelong, outside of Melbourne, is where I did a fair amount of growing up and that seemed like a good reason to visit and show Bender some special places. The clincher for Ben was that there are sensational beaches all along the coast. It's even called the Surf Coast from just outside the historic town of Queenscliffe all the way along the Great Ocean Road. Bells Beach at Torquay is where one of the major surf comps in Australia is held every year. There are loads of produce surprises, too. The biggest surprise of the trip was that I was under the impression that Bender and I were going to cater for a party my mother was hosting, but there was something cooking between Lozza and Bender that I wasn't aware of — and that was a surprise party for me! It was great fun, although much of the party itself is something of a blur. I'm sure someone will have some incriminating photographs to help me out, which are bound to be brought out at an inappropriate time. Oh well …

Byron Bay

BEN: I had been to Byron Bay with Dee, my partner, on many occasions before. This time was different, however. I was to meet Dee there and reconnect with our brand-new beautiful daughter, Ruby, who had flown from England to meet Dee's family for the first time. So, as you can imagine, as Curtis and I flew into Coolangatta (about an hour's drive away from Byron Bay), I was a little nervous. When I saw my two favourite girls in the airport, my heart melted. See, I'm just a big softie! Byron Bay is absolutely beautiful — it's where the rainforest meets the sea. The rich volcanic soils of the surrounding countryside mean sensational produce and spectacular scenery. Curtis and I found some great seafood, macadamia nuts and oils, excellent pork and some pretty special coffee, too. All this came together at a family gathering Curtis helped me cater for: a bloody fantastic barbecue on a deck overlooking a rainforest creek. How good is that? Hard to beat, I say.

Abrolhos Islands

Abrolhos Islands

Lobsters, Tuna and Boschettis

Ben O'Donoghue

If you point a boat due west from the coast of Geraldton in Western Australia, two or three hours later you'll run smack bang into the Abrolhos Islands. I reckon the description 'island' flatters them, as they're in fact flat coral plateaus, less than a metre or two above sea level, mostly devoid of vegetation. That's what's left of most of the islands after the British took Chinese workers there to remove rich guano more than a century ago.

The Abrolhos is rich in maritime history, too. More than sixty sailing ships have smashed into the coral reefs. The most famous shipwreck, but by no means the first, was the Dutch vessel *Batavia* in 1629. Driven forward at a great rate of knots by the Roaring Forties from the Cape of Good Hope in South Africa, the *Batavia* (like all the others shipwrecked) left its turn north to head for the Spice Islands of Indonesia too late. What followed after the ship broke apart on the reefs was mutiny and massacre: 125 men, women and children were slaughtered in drunken, sun-crazed binges. Captain Pelsaert escaped in a boat and rowed 1600 kilometres (1000 miles) north to Batavia (now Jakarta). Remarkably, he made it. He then returned with a platoon of soldiers to sort out the mutineers. Having survived six months on these islands, it probably means the mutineers were the first unofficial European settlers in Australia.

The name Abrolhos apparently comes from the Portuguese 'Abrios Oi-os', which means, 'keep your eyes open'. So much for the short history lesson!

Our 55-kilometre (35-mile) trip to the Abrolhos from Geraldton, which took a little over three hours, was uneventful, if a little rough. Our 16-metre (50-foot) converted tuna fishing vessel, with Captain Murray stoically at the helm, ploughed through the oncoming swell, spraying Curtis and me until we were soaked. But we couldn't feel too sorry for ourselves because we knew that in the early days, fishermen would come to the island in all weather in open sail-rigged dinghies!

North Island

Wallabi Group

East Wallabi Island

Beacon Island

Webbe Hayes Fort x

West Wallabi Island

x *Wreck of the Batavia*

INDIAN OCEAN

Easter Group

Leo's Island

Rat Island

Suomi Island

Wooded Island

Basile Island

Gun Island

Middle Island

Pelsaert Island

Pelsaert Group

Off in the distance we caught our first glimpse of the islands, low and flat on the horizon. They looked surreal, a little like a mirage. The waters surrounding the Abrolhos are as clear as crystal, and the reefs and fish schools are seen through the jade and sapphire waters. Pods of dolphin frolic, seals and sea lions sunbake and giant manta rays loll about in the shallows. The ocean here is a constant 22°C/72°F all year round, which means that the lobsters love it, tropical fish abound, and the reefs of coral thrive to rival the Great Barrier Reef in beauty. That means sharks, too, but more about that later.

We headed off to the Abrolhos because this is one of the main lobster fisheries on the west coast. One hundred and fifty licensed fishermen are allowed to take up residence on just twenty-two of the 122 islands that stretch nearly 100 kilometres (60 miles) in length. Crude shacks (or camps as they're called) are their homes for the five months of the season, and work is why they're here. Without an invitation, it's simply not possible to stay on the islands. During the annual season around 10,000 tonnes of western rock lobster are caught, many ending up on fine dining tables around the world.

We moored at one of the many jetties on Basile Island, one of the islands in the Southern Group, which boasts about twenty camps. Basile was first settled by Italian fishermen, and the names of the second- and third-generation rock lobster fishermen and women are evidence of that. Some of the other islands have built a pub or a community hall for the residents; on Basile Island they built a little church. The Archbishop of Geraldton visits and holds mass there twice a year.

On the island we were met by Pia Boschetti. Pia's father first came to the Abrolhos in the 1950s. Today Pia runs the family's pearl farm; sister Erica runs the family's tuna and swordfish fishing arm; and brother Michael fishes for lobster and trawls for school fish from his huge modern boat.

With so many of the Boschetti family there, I thought it would be nice to hold a family dinner and invite a few of the other people we met. That meant we'd need some food and, as fresh is best, we headed off in a jetboat to a secret spot on one of the islands that Murray Davidson knows. The jetboat is flat-bottomed so we were able to take short cuts across reefs where there was maybe only half a metre of water. This means that the lobster pots can be placed in otherwise inaccessible waters, especially close in where the swell is breaking over the reef. It's the most dangerous place for a boat to be and where lots of rock lobsters like to live. Just at the point the waves break is where the pots are lowered by rope. Their spots are marked by blue floats. Hauling the pots up into the boat can be quite heavy work if you have a few hefty lobsters inside!

On the way out to the secret spot, Murray asked if we'd like to go for a surf. Curtis and I were stoked and the waves Murray showed us were fantastic. We couldn't wait to get into the water, but as we were getting into our wetties, I glanced over the side just as three tiger sharks slid by. This is not a fisherman's story — they were huge, bloody huge and, as neither of us is crazy, we decided discretion was the better part of valour. After all, the place is not called Bitey Holes for nothing!

We also had a chance to drop a fishing line with a lure. The fish around the Abrolhos are amazing. We think Curtis hooked a big fighting Spanish mackerel — his fishing rod bent and the reel screamed like crazy before there was a crack! and the line snapped, letting the fish swim away in triumph. Spanish mackerel grow to over a metre (three feet) in length here. I left my line in and soon had a strike, too — a lovely coral trout. Anywhere else in the world it would have been a pretty big fish but here it was a tiddler in comparison to the other fish we'd seen, so we threw it back.

Murray said he'd show us a good-sized fish, so we made a detour into his camp. In the water beside the wharf he swished around a few leftover lobster shells. It wasn't long before a large bald-chin grouper appeared. This, Murray told us, was Pete, his pet, who'd been coming around for several months, striking up a friendship. Pete was no ordinary fish. Before he'd feed, he'd lift his head out of the water and take a good look at Murray and me. Then, after he'd eaten the leftovers, he would swim in a circle and float on his back to let Murray and me scratch his stomach, just like a cat or dog.

We eventually arrived at the secret island after our surfing and fishing detours. Every part of the surface of every coral face above and below the water we could see was covered with oysters! Unbelievable. The locals take a screwdriver with them, jemmy off the top shell, scoop the oyster into it with an oyster knife, squeeze over a little lemon and slurp it down. These are the freshest oysters I have ever tasted and they were bloody brilliant. As always with seafood, the simpler you treat the produce, the better. That was certainly the case here. If I'd had a cold bottle of Riesling, I reckon I could have spent the day there. Heaven!

The downside was that, as we couldn't prise the whole shell off, there was no way to safely and hygienically transport these plump little beauties back to camp. So we had a few more for luck, then sat down to have a think.

Pia got on the phone to Erica, who has boats fishing further out to sea near the continental shelf. Erica had a boat on the way into port at that moment so we ordered a fresh tuna from her and headed back to camp. The thought of a full fresh tuna was enough to send me into a spin of recipe ideas and taste combinations. By the time we'd reached the jetty I knew exactly what I was going to do. So did Curtis, but he needed one further ingredient that we didn't have — fresh tomatoes.

When the Chinese workers were here they brought with them numerous vegetables and plants. These days, after the rains, descendent tomatoes self-seed and self-sow in the crevices of a few small islands. Murray knew just where to look. Again we climbed on board the jetboat and took off at a great rate of knots. Not long afterwards we pulled up at an island. Murray jumped onto the beach and we duly followed. Not long into our walk, there they were: small, plump, red and pure — just as they would have grown more than a century before when they were first brought to these islands.

Back on dry land I was introduced to Perry Minissale. (Everyone on Basile Island has an Italian name and heritage.) Perry's a great guy and he showed us how he puts his catch into a holding pen to await the arrival of the supply boat, which takes the catch back to the mainland. Perry's pride and joy is Melissa, a painted mermaid that has been passed around between the fishermen who live on the islands. Perry lives alone out there. Except for Melissa that is.

At dinner, we not only had a sensational meal but it was accompanied by one of the most spectacular sunsets I have ever seen. According to the locals, 'That was nothing, you should have seen the sunset last week!' The dinner was a resounding success and even though our guests have been eating their produce for generations, we were still able to surprise them with new tastes, combinations and textures. I was stoked, especially by the comments made by Bert, Pia and Erica's dad.

What really impressed me about these islands was the fact that there are quotas and enforceable rules in place to ensure that this environment stays absolutely pristine and pure. The rock lobsters that leave here carry the Marine Stewardship Council tag, which means that they are from a certified sustainable environment — a great endorsement. The best specimens are kept alive and flown first class around the world to end up being served fresh at the best tables.

While Pia, Erica and Michael are second-generation Abrolhos Island workers, this attitude to long-term sustainability ensures that there will be the same opportunities for their children and their children's children. I reckon that's bloody great!

Rock oysters with Champagne jelly

What can I say about oysters and Champagne? I like to eat such exquisite seafood very simply and this is a match made in heaven. Champagne and wines can be turned into jellies so simply. For instance, Madeira works beautifully with chicken liver parfait. All this means is that you can now enjoy in food what you usually enjoy out of a glass.

SERVES 4

24 rock oysters (any oysters will do),
    freshly shucked
300 mL/10½ fl oz Champagne
3 gelatine leaves
1.5 kg/3 lb 5 oz rock salt
200 mL/7 fl oz water
1 cup loosely packed watercress

1. Remove the oysters from their shells and place in a bowl with their juices. Cover and keep in the refrigerator. Clean and dry the shells.

2. Pour the Champagne into a saucepan and place over a low heat to warm. Put the gelatine leaves in a bowl and cover with cold water. When softened, squeeze dry with your hand and add to the Champagne. Heat, stirring, until the gelatine dissolves. Remove from the heat.

3. Slightly moisten the rock salt with the water and spread on a tray large enough to take the oysters. Place the oyster shells on top so that they are sitting level. Pour enough Champagne into each shell to half fill. Chill in the refrigerator until set.

4. Chill any remaining jelly in a small container in the refrigerator, too. Once set, break up this jelly using a fork.

5. Place 3–4 leaves of watercress at the back of each shell. Place an oyster on the jelly and then spoon a small amount of the broken-up jelly at the back of the oyster shell.

Curtis Stone

Abrolhos Island rock oysters

We had the opportunity to grab some local rock oysters, and the residents had pointed out a clump self-seeding bush tomatoes, so it occurred to me to put a twist on a dish I do as Head Chef at Monte's in London.

SERVES 4

48 rock oysters (any oysters will do), opened

Dressing
500 g/1 lb 2 oz cherry tomatoes, cut in half
2 teaspoons chopped thyme
1 teaspoon chopped flat leaf parsley
½ teaspoon chopped tarragon
1 garlic clove, crushed
salt and freshly ground black pepper
1 tablespoon HP sauce
1 tablespoon sherry vinegar
2 teaspoons lime juice
tabasco sauce, to taste
4 tablespoons light olive oil
1 tablespoon freshly grated horseradish, to garnish

1. Ensure that the oysters are detached from their shell. Cover and keep chilled until ready to serve.

2. To make the dressing, place the tomatoes in a bowl with the thyme, parsley, tarragon and garlic, and season with salt and pepper. Set aside to marinate for 30 minutes. Transfer to a food processor and whiz until pulped, then strain through a sieve to extract the juice. Mix this with the HP sauce, vinegar, lime juice and tabasco sauce, then whisk in the olive oil. Chill before serving.

3. Arrange the oysters on crushed ice to keep them cold, and spoon over enough dressing to cover each oyster. Garnish with a little horseradish, and serve at once.

Tuna ceviche with aromatic salad

Buy a nice fresh piece of tuna from your fishmonger. Things to look for are a deep red colour, a firm smooth flesh that doesn't appear dull or watery and the cut surface should have a rainbow-like shimmer across it. Always have a smell; it should be fresh and a little salty.

SERVES 4–6

Marinade
juice of 5 limes
1 teaspoon sesame oil
1 tablespoon palm sugar*
1 tablespoon soy sauce
1 tablespoon coconut milk

Garnish
200 mL/7 oz vegetable oil
100 g/3¹/₂ oz Thai pink shallots (Asian
    shallots), finely sliced lengthways
3 garlic cloves, finely sliced lengthways

Salad
3 loosely packed cups frisée; purple basil
    leaves; curly endive, smaller inside
    leaves; mint; baby basil leaves
leaves of 1 bunch fresh coriander
500 g/1 lb 2 oz fresh tuna
2 avocados, diced
salt and freshly ground black pepper
1 teaspoon lemon juice

* Available at specialist Asian food shops.

1 To make the marinade, mix all the ingredients together in a ceramic bowl.

2 To prepare the garnish, heat 150 mL/5 fl oz of the oil in a small pan. Fry the shallots and garlic separately until golden. Be aware that the colour will increase after they have been fried. Remove with a slotted spoon and drain on kitchen paper. Cool and reserve.

3 Rinse and drain the cress, endive, mint, basil and coriander leaves. Transfer to a bowl, cover, and place in the refrigerator, until required. Using a very sharp knife, neatly cut the tuna into 1 cm/¹/₃ in slices. Place in the marinade, covering all the slices well, and leave for 5 minutes. Season the avocados with salt and pepper and toss with the lemon juice.

4 Gently drain the tuna, then arrange on a serving plate. Top with the avocado and drizzle over a little of the remaining oil. Toss the last of the oil with the cress and coriander and arrange on top of the avocado.

5 Grind the fried shallots and garlic with ¹/₂ teaspoon each of salt and sugar in a mortar and pestle to give a crumbly texture. Sprinkle over the salad and serve at once.

Rock lobster tagliatelle with fennel and truffle oil

The Abrolhos Islands produce some of the best rock lobsters in the world and, from my experience cooking overseas, I've yet to taste a lobster to match these. I like to use fresh truffles at work but here truffle oil works well; just don't use too much! This recipe is a special occasion dish.

SERVES 4

2 baby fennel bulbs
4 live rock lobsters (any lobster will do),
 weighing 500 g/1 lb 2 oz each
75 g/2³/₄ oz unsalted butter
4 drops of truffle oil
450 g/1 lb fresh tagliatelle
juice of 2 lemons
salt and freshly ground black pepper

1 Put a large pot of salted water on to boil.

2 Discard the tough outer leaves of the fennel bulbs, reserving the green feathery tops for garnish. Slice the bulbs into thin wedges 1 cm/¹/₂ in thick on the outside edge. Reserve.

3 Place the lobsters in the boiling water. When the water returns to the boil simmer for 8–10 minutes. Remove the lobsters with tongs and keep the water simmering. When cool enough to handle, separate the head from the body and remove the meat from the tail. Dice and reserve. Using a spoon, scoop out all the flesh and coral from the head. Force this through a sieve into a small saucepan. Mix with 3–4 tablespoons of the simmering water and add the butter. Place on a low flame to melt the butter and heat through. If the sauce is too thin, continue cooking until it reduces.

4 Meanwhile, put the fennel wedges and the pasta into the boiling water to cook. Add the oil to the sauce, and lemon juice to taste. Season with salt and pepper. Drain the fennel and pasta when it is al dente and return to the pan. Add the reserved lobster meat and pour in the sauce. Toss to coat. Serve with a sprinkling of chopped fennel tops.

Char-grilled sardines with borlotti bean salad

This is a dish that needs to be eaten in the sun. I first ate sardines grilled like this in the south of France, sitting outside near the water. They eat particularly well with borlotti beans. This is really healthy food, and is just right for the Australian climate.

SERVES 4

Marinade
finely grated zest of 2 lemons
1 tablespoon chopped thyme
10 garlic cloves, crushed
2½ tablespoons olive oil

8 large sardines
400 g/14 oz fresh borlotti beans in the pod, shelled
500 mL/18 fl oz chicken stock
2 vine-ripened tomatoes
1 cup finely chopped flat leaf parsley
5 garlic cloves, crushed
finely grated zest of 2 lemons
finely grated zest of 2 limes
finely grated zest of 1 orange
75 mL/2¾ fl oz extra virgin olive oil
sea salt and freshly ground black pepper

❶ Mix all the marinade ingredients together.

❷ Fillet the sardines, leaving them joined at the tail. Place in a flat dish and coat with the marinade. Cover and refrigerate for 12 hours.

❸ Place the beans in a saucepan with the chicken stock. Bring to the boil and simmer until soft, 25–30 minutes. Remove from the heat and allow to cool in the stock.

❹ Core the tomatoes and cut a cross on their tops. Plunge into a pot of boiling water for 10–12 seconds. Remove and cool in iced water for 1 minute before peeling. Squeeze out the seeds and dice the flesh. Place in a large bowl. Drain and rinse the beans, and combine with the tomatoes.

❺ Combine the parsley, garlic and the lemon, lime and orange zest. Stir in the oil and season with salt and pepper. Toss half through the bean and tomato salad. Pile the salad in the centre of four serving plates.

❻ Preheat a char-grill to very hot. Grill the sardines for 2 minutes on the skin side, then turn and cook for a further 30 seconds. Arrange two sardines per serving in a cross on top of the salad. Serve, drizzled with the remaining parsley dressing.

Curtis Stone

Barbecued rock lobster with garlic butter and béarnaise sauce

I simply love cooking with a fantastic creature like lobster. The Canadian and European lobsters are brilliant to use, and would work perfectly with this recipe. The important thing to remember when cooking lobster is that the water must not be too hot. Around 70°C/160°F is perfect. This temperature will allow the lobster meat to relax as it cooks.

Whenever I cook with lobster, I feel privileged to be using such first class ingredients, so I always treat these ingredients with the respect they deserve.

SERVES 4

2 small carrots, roughly chopped
2 stalks of celery, chopped
1 leek, sliced into chunks
1 lemon, roughly chopped
1 head of garlic, unpeeled, roughly chopped
1 onion, roughly chopped
2 green rock lobsters (any lobster will do),
*   weighing about 1 kg/2 lb 4 oz each*
200 g/7 oz garlic butter (see recipe opposite)
5 tablespoons béarnaise sauce
*   (see recipe opposite)*
chervil sprigs, to serve

1 Place the carrot, celery, leek, lemon, garlic and onion in a large saucepan, place over a moderate heat and bring to 70°C/160°F, a very slow simmer. Add the lobsters and poach for 5–8 minutes, depending on their size. Remove from the water and rest for 5 minutes.

2 Preheat the barbecue. Using a large knife, split the lobsters in half lengthwise. Remove the meat from the tail and slice into smaller pieces. Pipe about 2 tablespoons of garlic butter into the shells. Replace the lobster meat, then pipe the remaining butter over the top.

3 Transfer the tails in their shells to the hot barbecue. Close the lid and cook for 4–5 minutes. If the barbecue has no lid, cover the tails loosely with foil. Remove from the heat and spoon béarnaise sauce over the top. Garnish with chervil for serving.

continued opposite...

Curtis Stone

Garlic butter

250 g/9 oz unsalted butter, softened
1 tablespoon finely chopped shallots
    (eschalots)
4 garlic cloves, crushed
2 teaspoons finely chopped flat leaf parsley
1 teaspoon pastis, such as Pernod
salt and freshly ground black pepper

1 Mix the butter in a bowl with the shallots, garlic, parsley and pastis, and season with salt and pepper. Spoon into a piping bag fitted with a wide nozzle.

Béarnaise sauce

2 shallots (eschalots), chopped
5 white peppercorns
250 mL/9 fl oz dry white wine
500 mL/18 fl oz white-wine vinegar
4 sprigs of tarragon
4 free-range egg yolks
150 g/5½ oz clarified butter
salt and freshly ground white pepper
20 tarragon leaves, finely chopped

1 To make the reduction, place the shallots, peppercorns, wine, vinegar and 2 sprigs of tarragon in a saucepan and bring to the boil. Simmer for 20 minutes, or until reduced by three-quarters. Add the remaining sprigs of tarragon, then remove from heat. Cool, then chill in the refrigerator until cold. (This can be kept for 1 week.)

2 Strain the reduction. Place 2 tablespoons in a stainless steel bowl and add the egg yolks. Place the bowl over a pan of simmering water and whisk vigorously. Continue whisking until the mixture thickens to form a light, foamy sabayon. Remove from the heat.

3 Melt the butter, slowly pour it into the sabayon in a steady stream, whisking continually. Season to taste with salt and pepper. Line a coarse sieve with a piece of muslin and push the sauce through into a bowl.

4 Mix the remaining tarragon leaves through the sauce.

Curtis Stone

Coral trout poached in milk, lemon, basil and white wine

This is great served with creamy mashed potato or pea purée, or, as I do at the restaurant, with potato and ricotta dumplings (see following page), which are bit like gnocchi.

SERVES 4

1 tablespoon vegetable oil

4 fresh coral trout (or use sea bass or scorpion fish) fillets, weighing about 180 g/6^1/$_2$ oz each

salt and freshly ground black pepper

freshly grated zest of 1 lemon

1 dried chilli

1 garlic clove, finely sliced

125 mL/4^1/$_2$ fl oz dry white wine

500 mL/18 fl oz skim milk

2 tablespoons mascarpone cheese

4 tablespoons chopped basil

❶ Warm the oil in a saucepan large enough to accommodate the fish fillets in a single layer. Season the fillets with salt and pepper and place in the pan. Seal on both sides over a low heat, without colouring the flesh. Add the zest, chilli and garlic, and fry gently to allow the flavours to develop, 1–2 minutes.

❷ Add the wine and milk, increase the heat and bring to the boil. Reduce to a very gentle simmer and cover, with the lid gaping slightly. Poach the fillets until just cooked through, 4–8 minutes, depending on their thickness. When done, the flesh will flake when pressed gently. The sauce will appear slightly curdled. Remove from the heat and transfer the fish to warm serving plates. Add the mascarpone to the pan and stir into the sauce. Taste for seasoning and add the basil at the last minute. Serve the trout with plenty of sauce spooned over the top.

Ben O'Donoghue

Potato and ricotta dumplings

I like to call these dumplings rather than gnocchi because they contain a filling.

SERVES 4–6

500 g/1 lb 2 oz floury potatoes, scrubbed
1 large free-range egg
salt and freshly ground black pepper
freshly ground nutmeg, to taste
about 100 g/3½ oz plain flour
75 g/2¾ oz ricotta
1 tablespoon chopped basil

1 Boil the potatoes in their skins until cooked through, about 30 minutes. Drain and peel while hot. Press through a sieve into a large bowl. While still hot, add the egg, beating lightly until combined. Season with salt, pepper and nutmeg. Gradually incorporate the flour, stopping once a firm but light dough forms. Knead until just smooth, 30 or so seconds.

2 Mix the ricotta with the basil. Roll the dough out onto a floured surface to a thickness of 3 mm/⅛ in. Using a cookie cutter or an upturned glass, cut out 5 cm/2 in circles. Place a small teaspoonful of the ricotta mix into the centre of a circle and cover with another circle of dough. Press the edges to seal.

3 Bring a large saucepan of salted water to the boil. Cook the dumplings, a few at a time, until they float to the surface, about 1 minute. Remove with a slotted spoon and serve with the Coral Trout (see previous page).

Ben O'Donoghue

Barbecued hot and sour tuna escalopes

This quick and easy way of marinating fish is perfect for a summer barbecue, however, it is also lovely to pan-fry indoors. This marinade is also great for prawns and most firm fish.

SERVES 4

Marinade
2 tablespoons chopped shallots (eschalots)
2 tablespoons chopped garlic
2 tablespoons chopped ginger
2 tablespoons chopped chilli
*   (depending upon heat of chilli)*
2 tablespoons crushed lemongrass
zest and juice of 1 lime
2 tablespoons chopped mint
2 tablespoons chopped basil
2 tablespoons chopped coriander

4 tuna escalopes, weighing about
*   150 g/5^1/$_2$ oz each*
1 tablespoon olive oil
mixed salad leaves, to serve

1 To make the marinade, place all the ingredients in a large bowl and mix well.

2 Add the tuna to the marinade and rub over the escalopes. Cover with plastic wrap and chill for 30 minutes.

3 Preheat the barbecue or grill. Add the olive oil to the bowl and toss to coat. Cook on a hot barbecue or flat grill plate until cooked through, about 45 seconds on each side. Serve on a bed of fresh salad leaves.

Tropical fruits poached in mango wine

Tropical fruits are perfect to eat in summer. I love poaching fruits. If you can't find mango wine you could use fruit juice or stock syrup of 1 L/1³/₄ pt water, 500 g/1 lb 2 oz sugar and the juice of 3 lemons with some puréed mango to your taste.

SERVES 4–6

1.5 L/2²/₃ pt mango wine
1 stick of cinnamon
4 kiwifruit, peeled
6 lychees, peeled
cheeks of 2 mangoes, peeled
1 small pawpaw, peeled, quartered and
    seeded
1 honeydew melon, peeled, quartered and
    seeded
10 cm/4 in piece of ginger, peeled
1 cup tightly packed mint leaves

1 Place all but 4 tablespoons of mango wine in a large saucepan. Add the cinnamon and bring to the boil. Add the kiwifruit, lychees, mango, pawpaw and honeydew melon. Lower the heat and simmer gently for 3–5 minutes. Remove the fruit with a slotted spoon and spread on a large platter to cool. In a mortar, pound the ginger and mint with the remaining wine. Leave to infuse.

2 Spoon out half of the poaching liquid and save for another use. Bring the remaining half to the boil and reduce to half a cup.

3 Slice the fruit and arrange on a serving platter. Drizzle the reduction over the top.

4 Strain the infused wine and pour over the fruit for serving.

Note: The excess poaching liquid can be made into a jelly. Soak 1 gelatine leaf per 100 ml/3 ¹/₂ fl oz of liquid in cold water until soft. Squeeze dry and stir into the warmed poaching liquid. Pour into moulds and set in the refrigerator.

Curtis Stone

Broome

Broome

Muddies, Pearls and Mangoes

Curtis Stone

Thanks largely to the pearling industry, which began in the early 1870s, Broome is a melting pot of many cultures: Chinese, Japanese, Malay, Pacific Islander and Aboriginal. As a result, Broome has become a harmonious fusion between the cultures and cuisines of the West and the East. This is what we expected before we arrived. What surprised us, though, was the natural fusion that has occurred between the European and Asian ways of life and that of the traditional values of the Australian Aboriginal people.

As we entered Broome, we took a drive through Chinatown. A collection of buildings and stores showed that the oriental influence is still very evident. My first impressions of Broome were of the heat and the colours. It is hot, tropical, a little humid, and this dictates the pace at which things get done. Here they call that 'Broome time'.

Colours, vibrant primary colours. The coastline is spectacular. The ocean is an iridescent, opal green. The sky is a rich, endless blue. The greens are tropical, bold and lush. And the soil is red, really red. Deep, dark ochre and red. It's spellbinding, too. No wonder people are drawn back here time and time again and others find it hard to leave.

Our Broome adventure really began after we met Baamba. Baamba's a local Aboriginal character. He's an actor, a singer, and a know-all about who's who and where to get everything. He's been married four times and has a heap of grandkids. He loves good food, so on that count alone we were destined to be good friends.

Baamba is in touch with his heritage and culture and was able to tell us so much about the traditional way of life, the basis of which is being in touch with nature and the environment. Simple things, such as knowing mud crabs don't come out from their mangrove lairs in a full moon, as their camouflage is rendered less than ideal, can mean the difference between a good

*INDIAN
OCEAN*

Willie Creek
Pearl Farm ■

BROOME ●

*Roebuck
Bay*

Great Northern Highway

feed and an empty stomach. As can essential things like where crocs hide, where turtles lay eggs and where water can be found in the desert.

Another thing we learned was that a bro (brother or close friend) is called a bubbli. After we'd proven ourselves, we too became referred to as bubblis. 'Hey bubbli!' was the favoured greeting.

We noticed the 'Broome time' phenomenon means that when you want to do something, that's the right time. When you want to leave, that's the right time to leave. When you want to eat, that's the right time to eat. I think in Spanish-speaking countries they have something similar called mañana.

Broome time is not only about clock time, they have their own seasons too: wet season and dry season. When it rains in the wet season, it's almost a solid wall of water. There's no point running for shelter, you'll be drenched within seconds, and you might as well pull off the road if you're in the car, as you'll be virtually driving blind. As suddenly as it begins, it's over. The seasons then break down further, into barramundi season (barra being one of the very best fish to eat) and mango season, for instance. Everyone in town also knows when it's high tide or low. In Broome, that's important to know because the tides dictate most activities, as there can be up to a 9-metre (27-foot) rise and fall. It's not an unusual occurrence for the unwary to park their car on the beach and come back hours later to find it washed away! Plus, the tides dictate when you go fishing: the best fishing is on the neap tide, when the variation between the high and low tide is at its minimum. This is real integration with the ebb and flow of nature. Not fighting it, but going with the current. That's part of the Aboriginal culture that the entire town and, probably, region have adopted. As a general observation, it may also be the reason why the Aboriginal people have been able to survive and prosper for thousands of years in such a harsh and unforgiving land.

We asked Baamba if we could get some mud crabs and he knew exactly where to take us. Catching mud crabs might sound like fun, but a clue to what it was really like is contained in the name. We waited until low tide and then headed out into the mud where the mangroves grow. Mud. Icky, sticky and knee deep. But if you catch your muddies, it's all worthwhile.

With the help of a long piece of wire — which is used to prod the mud until you detect it clicking on a shell and then to coax the muddy from its hole, being careful to avoid its nipping claws — we got the crabs into a bucket and back to dry land, ready for culinary inspiration.

Barramundi is a local native fish, popular throughout Australia. It has a superb firm flesh that poaches, grills or bakes beautifully. Baamba took us down to the town boat ramp where a bubbli of Baamba's had just docked his fishing vessel. Baamba 'hoied' his mate Milton and we clambered aboard. Luckily, they were just sorting the catch and among it were some fantastic fresh barramundi and threadfin salmon that we took with us.

On the town beach we caught sight of Pete's Noodle Bus. Malay-born Pete's quite famous around here and, after a snack, we decided to get some of his fresh noodles.

Broome's Cable Beach is famous for two things. The first is the Cable Station, built here in 1889, that was the terminus of the undersea cable link between Australia and Java. The second is camels, which visitors can ride along the beach at dawn and dusk. Some important points to know about camels are that they have very poor dental hygiene so their breath could remove paint and they can't see behind them, as Bender found out when one camel stepped on his foot. You should have seen him jump.

Another bubbli of Baamba's was Arno, who grows mangoes. Baamba was able to get us some plump and luscious mangoes which were perfect for Bender's dessert of Mango and Chilli.

Pearls, pearl shells and pearling have always been a part of the way of life in Broome. In fact, Baamba told us how in his dad's day the kids used to use found pearls as marbles!

Baamba arranged for us to go out and see how pearls are grown and harvested. We were whisked away by chopper along the glorious coastline to the Willie Creek Pearl Farm. Pearl farms are not as exotic as they sound. Basically, they are line after line of pearl shells suspended in the ocean from a rope, filtering the clean waters of the north-west, growing big and fat, and growing South Sea pearls that have been seeded inside. It's a long slow process, and the shells need to be pulled from the water every eight weeks or so and cleaned to avoid diseases. South Sea pearls are known as the 'queen of pearls' and Broome pearls are sold around the world. While the traditional Japanese oyster pearl produces pearls about 11 millimetres (about half an inch) in diameter, the larger South Sea pearls native to Australia can grow up to 18 millimetres and even, rarely, up to 21 millimetres (almost 2 inches)!

In the early days — the days of brass helmets and hand bellows — diving for pearls was a very dangerous job indeed. A walk in the local cemetery is proof of that. More than 600 Japanese alone, among the people of many nationalities drawn to Broome to work as divers, lost their lives on the job. In 1910, Broome was the pearling capital of the world. This first industry was based around pearl shell (mother of pearl), which was in demand for buttons, cutlery handles, walking stick handles and as inlay in swords and pistols. But in 1958, the advent of the plastic button virtually wiped out the industry.

We, however, were here for the pearl meat. This is very rare and, at around $100 a kilogram, is likely to stay at the curiosity end of the gastronomic table. The texture is fine, the colour light grey and, as we later find out, the meat tastes like a cross between abalone and scallop. It's not everyone's cup of tea and, personally, I'll stick to scallops, but it was fun.

Now we have our ingredients, let's get cooking.

Tian of fresh mud crab, avocado and tomato with lime mayonnaise

This is a perfect dish to prepare if you are out to impress. It's quite a formal dish and one that takes a little more time than most; however, it looks very impressive. If you are after a more casual approach, use all the same ingredients and make a salad instead — this way you will cut down your prep time but will still have the same great taste.

SERVES 4

Poaching liquid

4 L/7 pints water

1 carrot, cut into chunks

2 stalks of celery, sliced into lengths

1 head of garlic, unpeeled, roughly chopped

1 leek, cut into chunks

1 onion, chopped

8 white peppercorns

2 fresh bay leaves

1 sprig of thyme

1 live mud crab (any large crab will do), weighing about 1.5 kg/3 lb 5 oz

8 large beefsteak tomatoes, weighing about 250 g/9 oz

20 coriander leaves

juice of 1 lime

2 ripe avocados, finely diced

1 bird's-eye chilli, deseeded and finely chopped

1 teaspoon olive oil

5 tablespoons lime mayonnaise (see recipe page 64)

1 teaspoon tomato paste mixed with 55 g/ 2 oz plain mayonnaise, to garnish

sea salt, to sprinkle

❶ Place all the poaching ingredients in a large saucepan and bring to the boil. Simmer for 10 minutes. Add the crab and cut off the string, releasing the claws. Cook for 18–20 minutes. Drain and chill the crab, still in its shell, in the refrigerator.

❷ Bring a large saucepan of water to the boil. Core the tomatoes and cut a cross on their tops. Blanch for 10–12 seconds. Refresh in ice cold water and peel. Using a sharp knife, cut the outer flesh off the heart of each tomato in one piece; it needs to be at least 7 cm/3 in wide. Lie out flat and cut out a circle 7 cm/3 in in diameter. Repeat with the remaining tomatoes.

❸ When the crab is cold, extract all the white meat, ensuring that it is free from the shell. Place the meat in a bowl with the coriander leaves and half the lime juice. In another bowl combine the avocado, chilli and remaining lime juice.

continued over...

Curtis Stone

4 On a work surface, place a tomato circle inside a 8 cm/3 in cookie cutter with high sides. Spoon a quarter of the avocado mixture into the cutter, smoothing it on top with the back of a spoon. Spoon a quarter of the crab mixture on top and smooth the surface. Top with another tomato disc and brush with oil. Spoon a quarter of the lime mayonnaise in the centre of a serving plate and smooth it into a circle. Using a palette knife, transfer the tian to the centre of the mayonnaise. Gently remove the cutter, leaving the tian in shape. Repeat this procedure until tomato, avocado and crab mixture is used.

5 Place the tomato mayonnaise in a squeeze bottle and decorate the plate around the lime mayonnaise with dots of colour. Sprinkle the top of the tian with a little sea salt.

Lime mayonnaise*

1 free-range egg yolk
1 teaspoon Dijon mustard
1 teaspoon white-wine vinegar
1 teaspoon lime juice
125 mL/4$^{1}/_{2}$ fl oz peanut (groundnut) oil
salt and freshly ground white pepper

1 Place the egg yolk, mustard, vinegar and lime juice in a mini food processor and mix until smooth. With the motor running, slowly add the oil in a thin trickle to give a thick mayonnaise. If necessary, incorporate a little warm water at the end to give the right consistency. Season to taste with salt and pepper.

This recipe can be increased by up to four times without jeopardising the balance.

Curtis Stone

Barbecued pearl meat with agridolce dressing and a mint and eggplant salad

Agridolce is Italian for sweet and sour. I prepare this recipe with scallops in my restaurant in London — from what I remember, pearl meat is similar.

SERVES 4

Dressing
55 g/2 oz fresh breadcrumbs
30 g/1 oz blanched almonds
1 anchovy fillet
2 tablespoons orange juice
2 teaspoons caster sugar
15 g/ $^1/_2$ oz bitter chocolate (100 per
*   cent cocoa solids), roughly chopped*
4 tablespoons white-wine vinegar
125 mL/4$^1/_2$ fl oz cup water
salt and freshly ground black pepper
2 teaspoons olive oil

Salad
2 small eggplant (aubergine), thinly sliced
200 mL/7 fl oz olive oil, for shallow frying
1 cup loosely packed mint leaves,
*   torn if large*
1 teaspoon lemon juice

320 g/11$^1/_2$ oz pearl meat,
*   or fresh scallops, prawns or squid*

1 To make the dressing, toast the breadcrumbs and almonds in a dry frying pan until golden. Pound together using a mortar and pestle, or grind in a small processor, until fine. Put to one side. Grind the anchovy and orange juice with the sugar and chocolate until paste-like. Bring the vinegar and water to the boil in a small saucepan. Stir in the breadcrumb mixture, followed by the anchovy mixture. Reduce the heat and simmer for 5 minutes. Taste for seasoning and cool. Stir in the olive oil. It should be a loose dressing.

2 To make the salad, shallow-fry the eggplant in the oil until golden and crisp. Drain on kitchen paper. Toss with the mint, lemon juice and 2 teaspoons of olive oil.

3 Grill the pearl meat on a hot barbecue until just done, 20–30 seconds. Divide the eggplant and mint salad between four serving plates and arrange the grilled pearl meat on top. Drizzle over the dressing and tuck in.

Ben O'Donoghue

Mud crab and green papaya salad

This is a Thai-influenced salad, so it's not exactly original. David Thompson may give me a hiding for this effort—so please forgive me David.

SERVES 4

1 live large mud crab (any large crab will
    do), weighing about 1.5 kg/3 lb 5 oz

Dressing
2 garlic cloves
1/4 teaspoon salt
1 1/2 tablespoons dried shrimp*
3–5 bird's-eye chillies, seeded
2 tablespoons palm sugar*
juice of 3 limes
2 tablespoons tamarind pulp
2–3 tablespoons fish sauce

1 green papaya or under-ripe honeydew
    melon, peeled and finely sliced
leaves of 1/2 bunch of mint
leaves of 1/2 bunch of Thai basil
leaves of 1/2 bunch of coriander
2 kaffir lime leaves, shredded
1 stalk of lemongrass, trimmed
    and finely sliced across the stem

1 Put the crab into a large pot of salted cold water. Remove the claw ties, so its muscles can relax. Cover and bring to the boil. Cook at a very low simmer for 20–25 minutes, then transfer to a sink full of iced water to cool quickly.

2 Using a heavy, sharp knife or poultry shears, remove the top shell. Pick all the white meat from the body and legs, making sure that no shell is included. Reserve meat for the salad.

3 To make the dressing, pound the garlic, salt and dried shrimp in a mortar and pestle or a small processor. Add the chillies and pound until paste-like. Add the palm sugar, lime juice and tamarind pulp, and blend well. Add enough fish sauce to give a pourable consistency. The taste should be hot, sweet and sharp, but balanced at the same time.

4 Place the papaya in a bowl with the white crab-meat, mint, basil, coriander, kaffir lime leaves and lemongrass. To serve, add the dressing and toss lightly.

* Available at specialist Asian food shops.

Zuppa di baccalà

This classic soup from Venice can be as simple or complicated as you like. You can either buy the salt cod from a quality Italian deli or make it yourself*. By salting the cod you are drawing out the moisture and intensifying the flavour.

SERVES 6–8

900 g/2 lb salt cod*
1¹/₂ tablespoons olive oil
225 g/8 oz leeks, white part only, in
*   large slices*
freshly grated zest of 1 orange
1 sprig of thyme
1.2 L/2 pints fish stock
200 mL/7 fl oz water
225 g/8 oz potatoes, peeled and cubed
500 mL/18 fl oz double/thick cream
freshly ground black pepper
finely chopped chives, to garnish

❶ Soak the cod in cold water for 2–3 hours. Drain and cover with fresh cold water. Continue in this way, changing the water often, for at least 24 hours. Remove the skin from the fish and dice the flesh. Heat the olive oil in a large pot and fry the cod over a moderate heat for 5 minutes. Add the leek, zest and thyme and cook over a low heat without browning for 5 minutes. Add the stock and water and bring to the boil. Add the potatoes and simmer until tender, 10–15 minutes.

❷ Remove from the heat and allow to cool slightly. Transfer to a food processor and blend until smooth. Place a fine sieve over a clean saucepan and strain the soup. Don't discard the solids collected in the sieve: they should resemble a light purée or brandade and will be used to make quenelles. Cover and refrigerate.

❸ Add the cream to the soup and bring to a simmer. Season to taste with pepper.

❹ Using lightly moistened spoons, form a tablespoon of the fish reserved purée into an egg shape. Repeat until the purée is all used.

❺ To serve, ladle the soup into bowls. Divide the quenelles between the bowls and garnish each with a sprinkling of chives.

* It is best to prepare your own salt cod at home. Take 1 kg/2 lb 4 oz fresh fillet of cod and cover with rock salt. Leave in the refrigerator for 12 hours, then wash off the salt under rapidly running water for 30 minutes. If you are pressed for time, it is available at specialist delicatessens.

Curtis Stone

Barbecued king prawn skewers wrapped in prosciutto with mango and chilli

Being an Aussie I feel proud to say that we have the best prawns in the world. I have some really fond memories of prawns, whether it is eating them in a swanky restaurant in Melbourne or straight from a plastic bag on a pier, after buying some from a fish cooperative on the beach. Here is a simple take on how to throw another prawn on the barbie.

SERVES 4

16 green king prawns

1 large just ripe mango

8 thin slices prosciutto, sliced into
    halves lenghways

2¹/₂ tablespoons chilli oil

2 lemons, quartered

4 wooden skewers, soaked in water
    for 20 minutes

1 Peel and devein the prawns, leaving the tail and head intact. Peel the mango and cut the flesh into 2-cm/1-in square pieces. Place one piece of mango in the centre of a prawn. Wrap a slice of prosciutto around each prawn.

2 Preheat the barbecue or grill. Spear a prawn onto a skewer, starting at the tail and coming out close to the head. Add three more prawns to the skewer in this way. Brush with chilli oil. Repeat using the remaining skewers. Char-grill on a barbecue or grill for 1 minute on each side. Squeeze lemon juice over the top, remove from the barbecue, and serve.

Curtis Stone

Thai-style baby barramundi with wok-tossed noodles and greens

Barramundi is a variety of perch, so if you are not lucky enough to get your hands on some barra you can easily substitute perch. Deep-frying fish is a quick hassle-free way to cook — and it is not necessary to have a deep-fryer: you can use a wok or a large pan.

SERVES 4

Marinade

2 shallots (eschalots), finely chopped

3 garlic cloves, crushed

2 cm/1 in piece of ginger, grated

1 red chilli, deseeded and finely chopped

2 teaspoons finely chopped mint

2 teaspoons finely chopped basil

2 teaspoons finely chopped coriander

1 stalk of lemongrass, trimmed and
    finely chopped

1 tablespoon light soy sauce

about 3 cups vegetable oil, for
    deep-frying

4 x 200 g/7 oz fillets of
    baby barramundi, cut
    into 2 or 3 thin slices*

125 g/5 oz cornflour

1 head of broccoli, weighing about
    150 g/ 4^1/$_2$ oz

200 g/7 oz hokkein noodles

2 shallots (eschalots), sliced

2 carrots, peeled, canalled** and sliced

2 baby bok choy, halved lengthwise

2^1/$_2$ tablespoons light soy sauce

1^1/$_2$ tablespoons sweet chilli sauce

^{1}/$_2$ cup loosely packed coriander leaves, to serve

❶ Mix all the marinade ingredients together in a bowl. Add the fish fillets and marinate for 15 minutes at room temperature. Slice the broccoli stem thinly and reserve. Trim the head into twelve florets. Bring a large saucepan of salted water to the boil. Blanch the florets for 2–3 minutes. Remove with a slotted spoon and reserve. Drop the noodles into the pan and cook until softened, about 45 seconds. Drain.

❷ Put 2 teaspoons of the oil into a wok. Pour the remainder into a deep-fryer or a large heavy-based saucepan. Heat to a point where a cube of bread, when dropped in, browns in 15 seconds. Dust the marinated fish in cornflour. Deep-fry in batches until golden, 2–3 minutes, and drain on paper towels.

❸ Meanwhile, heat the oil in the wok and fry the broccoli slices, shallots and carrots for 15–20 seconds. Add the bok choy. When wilted, add the noodles, soy sauce and sweet chilli sauce. Toss until heated. Moisten with a little water, if needed.

continued over...

Curtis Stone

Thai-style baby barramundi with wok-tossed noodles and greens, continued...

4 Neatly pile the noodle and vegetable mixture in the centre of four serving bowls. Arrange the barramundi slices on top and position three broccoli florets around the edge of each. Sprinkle with coriander and serve at once.

* *Why not get the fishmonger to do this when you buy the fish.*
** *To canal the carrots, cut out troughs along their length, right around the perimeter.*

Curtis Stone

Mango with chilli and lime sugar

This interesting combination of hot, sweet and sour is common in Asian cooking. It's dead simple to prepare and it's a great way to finish a meal.

SERVES 4

4 ripe mangoes, peeled and sliced
2–3 dried bird's-eye chillies
2 tablespoons caster sugar
finely grated zest of 2 limes

1 Arrange the mango slices on a plate. Place the chillies and a little of the sugar in a mortar and pound to break up the chilli. Add the remaining sugar and the zest, and pound to incorporate the sugar and zest.

2 Sprinkle over the mango slices, or serve separately on the side for guests to help themselves.

Ben O'Donoghue

Pineapple and black pepper tarte Tatin

Tarte Tatin was invented in France at the beginning of the twentieth century by the Tatin sisters and was served at Maxim's in Paris, where it is now a permanent fixture on the menu. It is classically made with apples but pineapple also works well. The tarte takes a little bit of time to prepare, but it can be made well in advance and is easy to serve.

MAKES 1 TART

55 g/2 oz unsalted butter, softened
55 g/2 oz caster sugar
½ teaspoon coarsely ground black pepper
1 x 5-cm/2-in thick slice of pineapple, cored
55 g/2 oz pre-rolled puff pastry
good quality vanilla ice-cream, to serve

1. Press the butter over the base of a small blini pan* approximately 10 cm/4 in in diameter and at least 5 cm/2 in deep. Sprinkle the sugar on top.

2. Press the black pepper onto one side of the pineapple and place, pepper-side down, on the sugar. Cut the pastry into a circle 2 cm/1 in larger than the diameter of the pan. Place over the pineapple and tuck the edges down between the pan and the pineapple. Rest for 10 minutes.

3. Preheat the oven to 190°C/375°F/Gas Mark 6. Place the pan over a low heat for 3 to 5 minutes until you see the sugar bubbling up around the side of the pastry, start to colour and turn light brown. Transfer to the oven and bake for 30 minutes. Remove and rest for 10 minutes, then invert the pan onto a clean plate.

4. Serve with vanilla ice-cream.

* Blini pans are useful not just for this tart and for making blinis, but for making small pancakes, Yorkshire puddings and perfect fried eggs.

Banana, pecan and walnut hotcakes

I love the odd banana and some fantastic organic bananas are grown in Broome.

SERVES 6

175 g/6 oz plain flour
1 tablespoon baking powder
1 tablespoon caster sugar
60 g/2 oz chopped walnuts and
    pecan nuts
6 ripe bananas
1 large free-range egg
250 mL/9 fl oz milk
2 tablespoons dark rum
85 g/3 oz softened butter
double/thick cream, to serve
golden syrup, to serve

1 Sift the flour into a bowl and add the baking powder, sugar and half the nuts. Mash three of the bananas in another bowl. Add the egg, milk, rum and half the butter, mix well and add to the dry ingredients. Mix well to combine.

2 Heat a non-stick frying pan and melt a little of the remaining butter. Spoon the batter into the pan to give hotcakes of about 7.5 cm/3 in diameter — three at a time fit comfortably. Cook until bubbles appear on the surface and the bottom is golden brown. Flip over and cook for a further 1–2 minutes. Remove from the pan and keep warm. Continue in this way until all the batter and butter is used up.

3 Slice the remaining bananas and serve with the hotcakes, cream, a drizzle of golden syrup and the remaining nuts sprinkled over the top.

Ben O'Donoghue

Banana semifreddo

This is one of my favourite recipes using banana.

SERVES 4–6

10 free-range egg yolks
100 g/3½ oz warmed honey
3 tablespoons rum or banana liqueur
4 tablespoons caster sugar
3 large ripe bananas
5 egg whites
500 mL/18 fl oz pouring cream
200 g/7 oz dark chocolate, chopped
55 g/2 oz unsalted roasted peanuts (other
    nuts may be used), finely chopped

1 Line a loaf tin or a glass pudding bowl with plastic wrap and place in the freezer to chill.

2 Place the egg yolks in a bowl with the honey, rum and half the sugar. Place the bowl over a saucepan of simmering water and whisk until the mixture is light and fluffy, and doubled in volume.

3 Mash the bananas with a fork in a large bowl. Add the egg mixture and stir to combine. In a clean bowl, whisk the egg whites with the remaining sugar until stiff. Fold into the banana mixture. Whip the cream to soft peaks and fold into the banana mixture. Add half the chopped chocolate. Spoon into the lined mould and freeze until set.

4 Melt the remaining chocolate by placing it in a bowl over a saucepan of simmering water (don't let the bowl touch the water), or in a microwave oven. Unmould the semifreddo onto a serving plate. Using a spoon, drizzle half the chocolate over the top in a criss-cross pattern, then sprinkle with the peanuts. Drizzle the remaining chocolate over the top. Return to the freezer until required.

5 About 15–20 minutes before serving, transfer to the refrigerator to soften

Hunter Valley

Hunter Valley

Big Cellars, Balloons and Barrington Tops

Curtis Stone

The Hunter Valley is well known in Australia as a premium wine-growing area. The valley, being almost 200 kilometres (125 miles) in length, has an amazing array of agricultural produce, which is what drew us to have a look around.

My first impressions of the Hunter Valley were just how lush, green and delightful the scenery was. In places, it looks like parts of Wales, in others, like parts of Canada, yet it is all distinctly Australian: from the depth of colour in the sky and the unique purple colour of the distant hills to the laconic, dry humour of the country folk. Our journey took us the entire length of the Hunter, from Cessnock in the east to the spectacular Barrington Tops in the north-west. In some places it took us back in time, and in others it showed us what the future in food could be.

The passion and dedication of the producers we were lucky to meet was apparent. With these people at the helm, it's my opinion that the Hunter Valley will continue to grow and develop its reputation as a quality producer of wine, beef, lamb, cheese, goats, native fish, rabbits, mushrooms, game birds and poultry.

While back in London, I had seen some photographs of the Hunter region that were taken from a hot-air balloon. I thought this sounded brilliant, so I set the alarm one morning for 4.30, spent ten minutes banging on Bender's door to wake him (he's not exactly a light sleeper) and then we headed off to Cessnock airport. It was still dark at 5.30 am when we got there, but one small office had its light burning brightly and a number of other would-be aviators had already gathered outside. Ballooning sure is popular here, there were three flights going up that morning — in our balloon there were twelve passengers. They pack 'em in like they do on the London Underground.

Scone

Barrington

Rawdon Vale • • Barrington

Barrington Tops ○ Gloucester

■ *Trudgalong Farm*

• Muswellbrook

○ Dungog

Singleton •

Karuah ○

Maitland ○

Robert's at Peppertree ■

Pokolbin • ■ *Redgate Farm*

Cessnock • Nelson Bay ○

Tyrells Winery ■

● NEWCASTLE

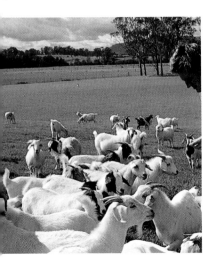

Ballooning was not exactly as I had expected. From the filling of the balloon on its side to the roar of the gas flame and the cavernous space of hot air, it was an experience and a half. When we were aloft, the view was spectacular. We drifted gently and peacefully (except for the occasional burst of the gas flame) over row after row of vines, across cattle-filled paddocks and over creeks and bushland. The landing was a little bumpier than I'd anticipated, but it must have been a regular occurrence for the cattle in our landing paddock merely ambled away as we approached. Breakfast at 7.30 am was well received and we wolfed down a huge plate of bacon and eggs. After all, we'd already been up for hours!

Our next stop was Redgate Farm where we were greeted by a quacking flock of plump ducks. Inside there were quite a few recently hatched fluffy ducklings and thousands upon thousands of quail. I think quails are quite finicky on the prep side, but boy, do they taste good. So that's what we chose.

Another stop was Trudgalong Farm, built on a dramatic rocky ridge overlooking its paddocks. Here chickens roamed freely, ducklings puddled near the dam, and in the bottom paddock was a flock of very contented goats. These goats are bred for the Sydney markets and for selected restaurants. Goat, or kid, is one of my favourite meats because of its rich taste. As well, the dams on the property are stocked with native silver perch, which are also specially bred and marketed. I was sent out with a fishing rod and some bait (and Bender's sceptical good wishes) and had a lucky catch. These perch are beautiful eating and similar in look to barramundi. Their natural environment is the safety of muddy water, so growers often put their fish into clear water for some days to purge them of their slightly muddy taste before market.

Barrington Tops is a World Heritage Wilderness area but is surrounded by some of Australia's finest grazing land and watered by cool pristine mountain streams. Taking the road towards Scone, we wound our way through a beautiful steep-sided valley and then abruptly turned upwards, heading towards the clouds. On the way down the other side of the rise, the vegetation became distinctly rainforest in nature. Giant tree ferns lined the roadside and vines hung from tall trees.

We headed towards Rawdon Vale and to Stobo House, an extraordinary old place built room by room over the years from stones found on the property. Here, in this pristine environment, they breed wonderful aged beef for the restaurant table. As we arrived, they were about to head out to bring in a mob of cattle. It was great to be back on a horse after quite a few years. Bender, on the other hand … well, looking at his style, I think from now on I'll call him Bob.

Grapes have been grown and wine produced in the Hunter since the 1830s. One of the earliest wineries was Tyrrell's, which was established in 1858. We visited and were lucky enough to get an insight into Australia's remarkable success in international wine exports from Bruce Tyrell, fourth-generation winemaker and voice of the Hunter wine region. Bruce took us into the oldest section of the winery. Old log beams hold up the ceiling, an ancient wine press stands idly in one corner, and row after row of old, large, dusty barrels sit on a hardened earth floor. The floor is sprayed with water every evening to keep the humidity up and the dust down.

By the main winery is the original slab-sided wooden hut that served as the Tyrrell pioneers' first home in the Hunter almost 150 years ago. The land was considered poor for pasture but great wines have come from the soils of this hilly property.

With the produce we had collected we held a luncheon in the gardens of Robert Molines' restaurant at Peppertree vineyard. Robert is originally from the south of France, born in the hills above Monaco. A great advocate of fresh, local produce, his training is from the classical French tradition, so I immediately felt at home in his kitchen. We ate at a table set on the lush lawn between a row of topiaried trees. An autumnal vineyard and a babbling brook next to a sweet white chapel completed the idyllic scene.

Silver perch en papiotte with braised cos lettuce

SERVES 4

Braised lettuce
1 carrot, finely chopped
1 onion, finely chopped
1 stick celery, finely chopped
55 mL/2 fl oz red wine
2 baby cos lettuce
500 mL/18 fl oz veal stock
2 fresh bay leaves
2 sprigs thyme
10 peppercorns

4 x 200 g (7 oz) fillets silver perch
   (or use sea bass or bream)
1 carrot, julienned
1 small bulb fennel, julienned
1 shallot (eschalot), finely sliced
1 leek, white part only, julienned
3 tablespoons Noilly Prat dry vermouth
3 tablespoons fish stock
salt and freshly ground white pepper
sprigs of flat leaf parsley, to garnish

1 To braise the lettuce, preheat the oven to 200°C/400°F/Gas Mark 7. Soften the carrot, onion and celery in a little olive oil in a roasting pan over a medium heat. Deglaze the pan with the wine. Cut the lettuces in half lengthways and place in the pan cut side down on top of the vegetables. Add the veal stock, bay leaves, thyme and peppercorns. Cover the pan with foil and put in the oven until soft, 25–30 minutes.

2 While the lettuce is in the oven, for each fish parcel take a piece of foil approximately 30 cm/12 in square and place the julienned carrot, fennel, shallot and leeks in the centre. Put a fish fillet on top and drizzle over some Noilly Prat and fish stock. Season with salt and pepper.

3 Fold the edges of the foil over the fish to form a tightly sealed parcel in the shape of a large pasty. Then put the foil parcels in a large dry pan over a high heat. The liquid inside the parcels will begin to boil, causing steam to expand the parcels. When the parcels have reached this stage, transfer the pan to the oven and cook for a further 4–6 minutes.

4 Once the lettuce is soft, remove from the roasting pan and strain the liquid. Reserve the liquid. Place half a lettuce in the centre of each plate.

5 Remove the foil parcels from the oven and open them, being careful not to burn yourself on the steam. Place the fish on the lettuce and garnish on top with the vegetables. Sauce with a little of the reserved liquid and garnish with a sprig of parsley.

Curtis Stone

Poached perch with garlic, ginger and spring onion

The farming of fish is an important part of a sustainable fishing resource that supplies both professional and domestic chefs. The important thing is that these aqua farmers produce their fish in the least intensive manner possible and re-create the fish's natural diet. In this way the final product is healthy and as close as possible to the qualities of a wild fish. At the fish farm we visited in the Hunter Valley this ethical approach was in practise and the results were in the tasting — bloody fantastic.

SERVES 4

Poaching liquor
100 g/3¹/₂ oz ginger
2 L/3¹/₂ pints water
10 spring onions, white parts only
2 tablespoons salt
5 tablespoons rice-wine vinegar

4 x 400 g/14 oz silver perch (or use
    sea bass or bream), cleaned

Dressing
2–3 garlic cloves, peeled
salt
about 5 tablespoons rice-wine vinegar
about 5 tablespoons peanut (groundnut) oil

4 tablespoons light soy sauce
green tops of 10 spring onions, finely sliced

1 To make the poaching liquor, peel the ginger, placing the trimmings in a stockpot. Grate the cleaned ginger and reserve for the dressing. Add the water, spring onions, salt and vinegar, and bring to the boil. Strain into a fish-poaching kettle or a baking tray large enough to take the perch side by side.

2 Place on a low heat and keep just under simmering point. Place the fish into the poaching liquor so that they are completely covered. Leave to cook gently for 15 minutes. They are done when a spine from the dorsal fin pulls out easily.

3 Meanwhile, make the dressing by placing the garlic and reserved ginger into a mortar. Add a pinch of salt and pound to a paste. Add enough vinegar and oil to make a dressing. This can also be done in a mini food processor.

4 Transfer the fish to warm plates. Drizzle the soy sauce over the top, followed by a little poaching liquor. Spoon the dressing over the fish and scatter over the sliced spring onion tops.

5 Serve with steamed rice.

Char sui pork with Asian vegetables

Char sui translates to barbecue pork and is a Cantonese specialty. The marinade is very easy to knock out. Not only can you use a fillet as I have done here, but anything from ribs to pork belly is suitable.

SERVES 4

Marinade
200 g/7 oz char sui paste*
1 tablespoon soy sauce
3 tablespoons honey
1 garlic clove, bruised
1 cm/$^1/_2$ in piece ginger, sliced

2 medium pork fillets

Vegetables
$^1/_2$ head broccoli, weighing about 250g/9 oz
1 zucchini (courgette)
1 carrot
$^1/_4$ each of a red, yellow and green
    capsicum (pepper)
1 tablespoon vegetable oil
1 Asian shallot (eschalot), sliced
1 small garlic clove, crushed
$^1/_4$ teaspoon grated ginger
$^1/_2$ head pak choy, shredded
2 tablespoons soy sauce
1 tablespoon oyster sauce
1 teaspoon sesame oil

❶ Mix all the marinade ingredients together in a ceramic or glass bowl and add the pork fillets, turning to coat. Cover with plastic wrap and marinate for 24 hours in the refrigerator.

❷ Preheat the oven to 180°C/350°F/Gas Mark 5.

❸ Remove the pork from the marinade and seal on all sides in a medium frying pan, 5–6 minutes. Transfer to a roasting dish and roast for 8 minutes. Remove and rest, covered with foil, for 3–4 minutes.

❹ Cut the broccoli, zucchini, carrot and capsicum into bite-sized pieces. Heat the oil in a wok and add the cut vegetables along with the shallot, garlic, ginger and pak choy. Stir-fry for 15–20 seconds. Add the soy sauce and oyster sauce and continue frying until the vegetables are al dente, 20–30 seconds. Stir the sesame oil through. Transfer the vegetables to serving bowls.

❺ Carve the pork diagonally into 1 cm ($^1/_2$ in) slices and arrange on top of the vegetables. Drizzle any juices from the roasting dish over the top and serve.

* Available from Asian specialty food shops

Curtis Stone

Grilled quail salad with speck, radicchio, red onion and lentils

SERVES 4

100 g/3^1/$_2$ oz puy lentils*
1 stick of celery, cut into 3 lengths
4 celery leaves
2 garlic cloves, peeled
juice of 1 lemon
3–4 tablespoons extra virgin olive oil
salt and freshly ground black pepper
1 medium red onion, peeled and sliced into
    5 mm/^{1}/$_4$ in rings
3–4 teaspoons balsamic vinegar
^{1}/$_4$ head radicchio, cut into thin wedges
4 large quail per person**
2 teaspoons thyme leaves
8 pieces thinly sliced speck
^{1}/$_2$ cup mint leaves
^{1}/$_2$ cup picked watercress
1–1^1/$_2$ tablespoons aged balsamic vinegar***

1. Rinse the lentils, then place in a saucepan and cover with cold water to a depth twice their volume. Tie the celery stick and leaves together and add to the water along with the garlic cloves. Bring to the boil and simmer until the lentils are tender, about 40 minutes. Discard the celery and garlic and strain. Place in a bowl, add the lemon juice and 1 tablespoon of oil and season with salt and pepper. Set aside and keep warm.

2. Heat a griddle plate or a ridged pan to medium and brush with olive oil. Cook the onion rings slowly so they become soft and sweet. Transfer to a bowl and toss with a teaspoon of olive oil and the balsamic vinegar. Brush the griddle with a little more oil and slowly cook the radicchio wedges until lightly browned. Season and add to the bowl with the onion. Keep warm.

3. Preheat the oven to 180°C/350°F/Gas Mark 5. Season the quails with salt, pepper and the thyme. Heat a frying pan to hot, add a little oil and quickly brown the quails and speck. Transfer to a roasting dish and roast for 10 minutes. Remove from the oven and drizzle with a little oil and balsamic vinegar.

continued over...

* Where puy lentils are unavailable, use green.
** If you're in luck, your butcher or poulterer might partially bone the quail. Otherwise, cut them in half lengthways.
*** If aged balsamic vinegar is too expensive, you can gently reduce normal balsamic in a small pan until thick, then allow to cool.

Ben O'Donoghue

4 Adjust the seasoning of the onion and radicchio mixture if required, then divide among four plates. Place a quail on top and divide the speck evenly between the servings.

5 In a bowl, mix together the mint and watercress leaves with the juices from the roasting dish. Spoon over the top of the quails. To serve, drizzle a ring of aged balsamic around the salad and a trickle of oil.

Ben O'Donoghue

Spiced loin of lamb with spinach and pine nuts

This is a different way of using spices. You are making your own curry paste and then infusing the food rather than overpowering the flavours. When using strong-flavoured ingredients I always prefer to control the amount.

SERVES 6–8

Sauce

1 tablespoon grape seed oil (or use vegetable, sunflower or rape seed oil)

2 kg/4^1/$_2$ lb diced lamb (from the shoulder)

2 shallots (eschalots), peeled and halved

8 sprigs of thyme

4 sprigs of rosemary

pinch of saffron

2 star anise

2.5 L/4^1/$_2$ pints lamb or beef stock

1^1/$_2$ tablespoons pine nuts

Curry-infused oil

1^1/$_2$ tablespoons cumin seeds

2 tablespoons coriander seeds

1 tablespoon fennel seeds

1 tablespoon turmeric

1^1/$_2$ tablespoons paprika

2 tablespoons grape seed oil (or use vegetable, sunflower or rape seed oil)

2 x 700 g/1^1/$_2$ lb rolled bone lamb loins

2 tablespoons butter

150g/5^1/$_2$ oz spinach leaves, washed

① To make the sauce, heat the oil to very hot in a large heavy-based pan. Fry the diced lamb in 3–4 batches over a high heat until golden brown, 5–6 minutes per batch. Add the shallots, thyme, rosemary, saffron, star anise and stock and bring to the boil. Cook at a rolling boil, skimming often, until the liquid is reduced by half, about 1 hour. Strain into a smaller saucepan. Reserve the lamb for a latter use. Bring the sauce back to the boil and reduce by half again, 15–20 minutes. Add the pine nuts.

② In the meantime, make the curry-infused oil. Toast the cumin seeds, coriander seeds and fennel seeds in a dry frying pan for 3–4 minutes, until aroma-tic. Transfer to a mortar and pestle, add the turmeric and paprika and crush to a fine paste. This step can be done using a spice mill. Transfer to a small bowl and stir in the oil. Brush all over the lamb and set aside.

③ Preheat the oven to 200°C/400°F/Gas Mark 7.

continued opposite...

Curtis Stone

4 Heat a large pan to very hot and add the butter and spinach all at once. Toss to coat the leaves and remove from the heat once they wilt. Strain off any excess liquid and return to the pan to keep warm.

5 Brown the lamb all over in a hot frying pan. Transfer to a baking dish and roast for 6 minutes for rare, 8 minutes for medium rare. Remove from the oven, cover with foil and rest for 3–4 minutes. Slice.

6 To serve, place the spinach in the centre of serving plates and arrange some lamb slices on top. Drizzle the sauce around the outside and serve.

Curtis Stone

Porterhouse pot-roasted with bay, garlic and red wine vinegar

This dish would be great with a lovely creamy purée of parsnips or some braised silver beet or Swiss chard.

SERVES 4–6

1 kg/2 lb 4 oz whole porterhouse
    (sirloin) beef
salt and freshly ground black pepper
2 tablespoons olive oil, for browning
55 g/2 oz butter
10 fresh bay leaves
4 garlic cloves, peeled and halved
375 mL/13 fl oz Cabernet Sauvignon
    vinegar

❶ Trim the fat on the piece of beef to about 2 cm/1 in thick. Using a sharp knife, cut a crisscross pattern at 1 cm/½ in intervals across the fat. Season lightly with salt, but add plenty of pepper. Heat oil in a large heavy-based flameproof pot. Add the beef and brown on all sides, leaving the fatty side until last. Reduce the heat and slowly brown the fat; at the same time you will be rendering it (reducing the fat content). Remove the beef from the pot and drain off the fat.

❷ Melt the butter in the pot until foaming, then add the beef. Add the bay leaves, garlic and 5 tablespoons of the vinegar. Moisten a piece of baking paper large enough to cover the pot. Push the damp paper down into the pot to rest on and cover the beef entirely. Simmer over a low heat until the vinegar reduces by half. Add a little more vinegar and when that reduces, add some more. Continue in this way until the beef is cooked to medium, 50–70 minutes. The sauce should never completely reduce because you are trying to create an emulsion (a creamy mixture of the beef fat and the vinegar). Add water, if necessary.

❸ Turn off the heat and rest for 10 minutes. Slice the beef and serve. Spoon a little of the sauce over the beef and garnish with the bay leaves and garlic.

Standing roasted veal rib with a fricassee of cabbage and mushrooms

SERVES 6

1 tablespoon olive oil

1 veal rib on the bone, weighing about
    1.2 kg/2³/₄ lb

¹/₂ Savoy cabbage

55 g/2 oz butter

2 garlic cloves, finely chopped

200 g/7 oz fresh ceps (or similar wild
    mushrooms), sliced

5 tablespoons pouring cream

2 teaspoons chopped chives

2 tablespoons finely chopped flat leaf parsley

1 Preheat the oven to 200°C/400°F/Gas Mark 7. Heat the oil in a large, heavy-based pan and seal the veal over a high heat until browned all over, 6–8 minutes. Season with salt and black pepper and transfer to a baking dish. Roast for 40 minutes.

2 Discard the outer leaves and core of the cabbage and finely slice the leaves. Bring a large pot of lightly salted water to the boil and blanch the leaves for 2 minutes. Drain, refresh in cold water and drain well.

3 Heat the butter in a separate pan and sweat the garlic without colouring over a low heat for 30 seconds. Add the mushrooms and sauté for 2 minutes, then remove from the pan.

4 Add the cabbage to the pan and cook until al dente, about 2 minutes. Return the mushrooms to the pan and add the cream. Cook, stirring once or twice, for 2–3 minutes. Stir in the chives and parsley, and season with salt and freshly ground black pepper.

5 Remove the veal from the oven and cover with foil. Rest for 10 minutes. Carve into slices at the table and serve over the cabbage and mushroom fricassee.

Curtis Stone

Chocolate bread and butter pudding

When it comes to English classics, one of my favourite things is the timeless bread and butter pudding. I have fiddled around with it a little and added some chocolate and some Baileys liqueur, which adds a little richness and gives it a lovely texture. I use brioche instead of bread, which already contains a lot of egg and butter, so there is no need to butter the bread. Croissants also work well as a substitute for bread.

SERVES 4

600 mL/1 pt double cream
200 mL/7 fl oz Baileys Irish Cream liqueur
150 g/5 ¹/₂ oz sugar
2 vanilla pods, split in half lengthways
9 free-range egg yolks
9 whole free-range eggs
10 slices brioche, each slice about
    1 cm/¹/₂ in thick
200 g/7 oz dark chocolate (70 per cent
    cocoa solids), chopped

1 Place the cream, Baileys, sugar and vanilla pods in a large saucepan and heat, stirring, until the sugar has dissolved. Remove from the heat and cool. Remove the vanilla pod.

2 Preheat the oven to 130°C/250°F/Gas Mark 1, and grease a shallow six-cup capacity ovenproof dish. Whisk the egg yolks and eggs together in a large bowl, and strain in the cream mixture. Whisk lightly to blend. Cut the brioche slices in half diagonally and arrange in the prepared dish in slightly overlapping layers. Pour the cream mixture over the top and leave for 10 minutes.

3 Melt the chocolate in a microwave oven, or by placing it in a heatproof bowl over a pan of hot water, making sure that the water does not touch the bowl. Pour over the top of the pudding. Place in a baking dish half filled with warm water and transfer to the oven. Bake until set and golden, about 50 minutes.

Curtis Stone

Pears baked in red wine and vanilla

Pears are a fantastic autumn fruit, plus they are cheap and readily available. They are particularly good baked, as a dessert. This recipe is very easy and looks great. While I was in the Hunter Valley, surrounded by some of the best wine in the country, I thought I'd take the opportunity to try a variation of the classic dessert made with Barolo that I once ate in Piedmont in Italy. Choose pears with a fine skin to ensure a better eating texture.

SERVES 4

4 ripe pears
55 g/2 oz unsalted butter
100 g/3¹/₂ oz caster sugar
2 vanilla pods, split in half lengthways
grated zest of ¹/₄ orange
500 mL/18 fl oz red wine (Cabernet)
4 tablespoons crème fraîche

1. Preheat the oven to 150°C/300°F/Gas Mark 3.

2. Wash and dry the pears, then cut a small slice from the bottom of each so it can stand upright. Smear the butter all over them and sprinkle with 2 tablespoons of the sugar.

3. Mix the remaining sugar with enough water (1–1¹/₂ tablespoons) to make a paste. Place in a heavy-based flameproof pot large enough to hold the pears upright. Heat until the sugar paste turns a light golden colour. Add the vanilla pods, zest and half the red wine. Place the pears upright in the pot and transfer to the oven.

4. Bake, spooning the red wine sauce over the pears at frequent intervals until the pear is soft and the syrup is reduced, about 45 minutes. Add more wine if the liquid reduces too much.

5. The pear is cooked when the flesh is soft and the outside slightly wrinkled. Remove from the oven and cool in the pot to room temperature. To serve, drizzle the syrup over the pears and add a spoonful of crème fraîche.

White chocolate cheesecake

This is a simple baked cheesecake that is fantastic served with fresh or poached berries. I don't make it with a traditional base, but instead line the tin with biscuit crumbs.

SERVES 4–6

*55 g/2 oz biscuit crumbs, made from Anzac,
   butternut or good chocolate biscuits
1 vanilla pod, split in half lengthways
250 g/9 oz white chocolate, chopped
250 g/9 oz crème fraîche
500 g/1 lb 2 oz cream cheese
4 large free-range eggs*

❶ Preheat the oven to 150°C/300°F/Gas Mark 3. Grease a 20 cm/8 in springform tin. Throw in the biscuit crumbs and roll the tin around to coat the sides. Leave the excess on the base in an even layer.

❷ Scrape the seeds from the vanilla pod into a bowl with the white chocolate. Heat the bowl over a pan of simmering water, don't let the water touch the bowl, until the chocolate melts. Fold in the crème fraîche and stir until smooth.

❸ Beat the cream cheese until soft and smooth. Add the eggs, one at a time, beating well after each addition. Fold in the chocolate mixture and mix thoroughly. Pour into the prepared tin. Bang the tin down on the bench to remove any air bubbles.

❹ Transfer the tin to a baking dish half filled with warm water. Bake until firm and golden brown, 50–60 minutes. Don't worry if the top does not colour very much; it is more important that the centre is cooked so that it wobbles, but doesn't crack. Rest for several hours to cool and become firm, then turn out and slice into wedges for serving.

Ben O'Donoghue

New Norcia

New Norcia

Cattle, Goats and Monks

Curtis Stone

We headed north from Perth along the Great Northern Highway to a monastery town called New Norcia. Bender had played Aussie Rules footy here as a kid so there were no surprises for him, but for me the first encounter was quite startling. In the middle of nowhere, a little piece of Spain appears to have been scooped up and laid out. There's history in every building and artefact. And living history, too, in the sheltered life the monks lead — life that has essentially not changed for centuries.

I'd read that in 1846 a group of Spanish Benedictine monks led by Bishops Rosendo Salvado and José Serra landed in Fremantle, Western Australia, and then walked 180 kilometres (112 miles) north to build a self-sufficient mission and orphanage which operated until 1973. Spanish Classical, Byzantine and Gothic buildings with internal court-yards were built in the stifling Australian heat. It's Australia's only monastic town and this is reflected in the amazing collection of religious art in its gallery.

New Norcia was most likely the site of Australia's first experience with Mediterranean cuisines. The monks' first task was the planting of an olive grove. The oil was used as medicine for wounds and stomach ailments, for hair care, and for holy purposes. Very useful even then! Today, Dom Paulino looks after the olive trees and also makes the monastery's olive oil in an ancient wheel press driven by whirring gears and pulleys. Little has changed in his world except that at ninety-three Dom Paulino gets about his grove on a bright yellow four-wheeled farm bike. He's been at the monastery since he left Spain almost seventy-five years ago. For the first fifty years he was the monastery baker. He only ever made one type of bread — a traditional big Spanish four-pounder. He estimates that he has made more than a million loaves in his time, all by hand.

New Norcia is now quite well known for its bakery, so we called in and met Kingsley Sullivan, who these days not only makes bread for the monks and the town, but has made New Norcia sourdough bread famous, too. The New Norcia Bakery also produces nut cake, pan chocolate and

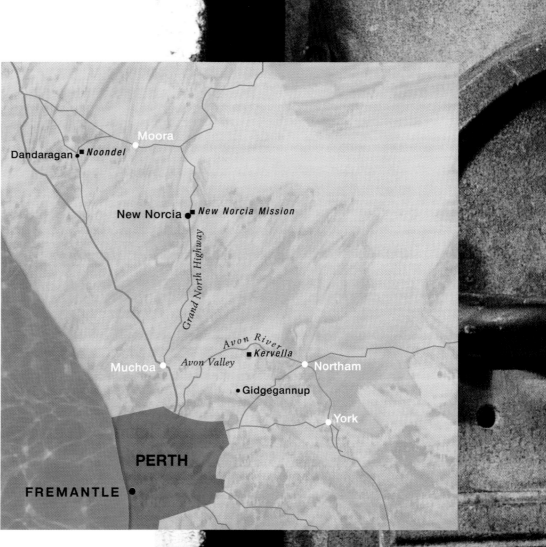

Dandaragan ■ *Noondel*

Moora

New Norcia ■ *New Norcia Mission*

Grand North Highway

Avon River

Kervella

Muchoa *Avon Valley* Northam

• Gidgegannup

PERTH York

FREMANTLE •

almond biscotti, all of which are sold around the world. The bakery has not changed much in almost 150 years and there's history in the very bricks themselves. The firebox still glows with logs of hot-burning jarrah, and the brick oven, as big as a small bedroom inside, is the perfect place to bake. Kingsley loves it. And he loves making bread. Broach the subject with him at your peril, lest he never stops talking about it, but that didn't stop me because I love people who are passionate about food and produce.

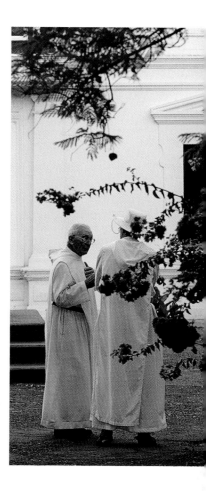

We asked if we could use the oven to cook in and Kingsley readily agreed. As it turned out, Ben and I ended up sweating off quite a bit of weight doing it. The temperature in there can reach more than 50°C/120°F at the height of summer; it's close to hell for those not used to it. The bakers, though, seemed perfectly at home. Once Bender and I were in there cooking, I began to feel there was a kind of link to the wood-oven kitchens of medieval times and a back-to-basics feeling that was really warming. I mean literally warming, too!

New Norcia was named after the Italian birthplace of St Benedict. Today, on the monastery's 10,000-hectare (25,000-acre) farm, they raise sheep and produce wheat, canola, grapes, honey, oranges, figs, plums, mandarins and quinces. Dom Chris, who we'd met earlier, had already promised us a leg of lamb from the monastery's flock of over 5000 sheep, and Kingsley had agreed he'd provide the sourdough bread. Bender said he'd like to cook the lamb with rosemary. As rosemary grows everywhere in New Norcia, a fresh bunch was easy to find near the church.

We called at the orchard behind the monastery, where we met Dom Stephen who gave us some oranges picked fresh from the trees. He suggested we walk down into the cellar, where we met well-known winemaker Nick Humphry. New Norcia also produces that other Mediterranean staple (along with the bread and olives) — wine, both red and white. We found Nick standing among rows of old and dusty barrels. These barrels are the basis of the monastery's solero system, which produces the famous liqueur Muscat that Nick grows and blends. Our 'blind' taste test was a wonderful experience.

During our chat with Kingsley we learnt about other interesting quality produce in the district: Kervella goats cheese and Dandaragan organic beef. That set us off on a quest to visit and learn more about them.

Gabrielle Kervella was once a violinist in the Western Australian Symphony Orchestra, but now, with her partner, Alan Cockman, she produces a range of award-winning goats cheeses, the demand for which across Australia far out-strips supply. The property is at Gidgegannup, high on a ridge overlooking the Avon Valley and the Avon River. Rocky and high, it is almost impossible to farm with traditional crops or stock. Goats, organically farmed, fit the bill. Gabrielle and Alan travelled to France to learn traditional techniques of goat rearing and cheese-making. They make frais (fresh cheese), some ash-covered to protect the cheese and to draw out the acidity, as well as a beautifully textured aged cheese that has developed a natural rind.

Dandaragan is not exactly next door, but in country Australia it's not unusual to travel more than an hour or two to do the shopping or just to drop in for afternoon tea. The farmhouse was built by convicts more than 150 years ago and the approach to farming was traditional for over 100 of those years. So the decision to go organic was not taken lightly. It means no chemicals for the land or the herd. All the meat is grown in the healthiest way possible, maximising food taste, integrity and pure goodness.

That evening back at New Norcia we prepared dinner in the monastery's baker's oven for the new friends we had met. We served our guests on the upstairs balcony of the Spanish-inspired New Norcia Hotel. With hundreds of galahs and parrots chiming in for the sunset chorus, we joined our guests for a memorable meal in a memorable setting as the retreating sun painted the horizon pink and orange.

The thing I found fascinating about the people I had met in this region is that all of them, no matter what they produced, seemed to be salt-of-the-earth types. They all have a refreshingly simple respect for the environment and their animals, and a real care and concern for the raw produce that ended up as a brilliant ingredients in our kitchen.

Farinata

For me these are the ultimate nibbly bits — a cool drink and a plate full of these crispy chickpea crepes with a simple flavouring just can't be beaten. They also make a great addition to an antipasto platter, or can be eaten just as a snack. The success of this recipe depends on the temperature of the oven and the pan — the hotter the better!

SERVES 4–6

300 g/11 oz chickpea (besan) flour
1 L/1³/₄ pints water
salt
about 125 mL/4¹/₂ fl oz olive oil

Topping
8–10 green yabbies or prawns, shelled,
    deveined and sliced
1 tablespoon rosemary leaves, coarsely
    chopped
freshly ground black pepper

1. Sift the flour into a medium bowl. Gradually stir in the water and mix to a very thin, lump-free batter. Set aside to rest for 30 minutes.

2. Preheat the oven to 250°C/500°F/Gas Mark 10. Place a handleless non-stick or cast-iron pan that has a seasoned bottom in the oven to heat to the same temperature. Season the batter with salt and stir in 1 tablespoon of the oil. Mix well. Carefully remove the pan from the oven and add enough olive oil to just cover the bottom. Pour in just enough batter to cover the pan in a thin layer. Scatter some yabby or prawn pieces on top, and sprinkle with a little rosemary and black pepper.

3. Place in the oven and cook for 8–10 minutes, or until the edges are brown, the centre cooked and the bottom crisp. Transfer to a wire rack and repeat with the remaining ingredients.

4. Serve hot — it does not matter if it breaks up!

Ben O'Donoghue

Focaccia

The addition of beer stimulates the yeast and adds flavour to the bread. If not needed immediately, one portion of the dough may be wrapped in plastic wrap and frozen for future use.

MAKES 2 FOCACCIA 28 X 38 CM (11 X 15 IN)

500 g/1 lb 2 oz semolina flour
625 mL/22 fl oz cups tepid water
30 g/1 oz fresh yeast or 15 g/¹/2 oz
*   dried yeast**
100 mL/3¹/2 fl oz beer
500 g/1 lb 2 oz bread flour**
1 tablespoon salt
125 mL/4¹/2 fl oz olive oil
coarse sea salt and freshly ground
*   black pepper*

Toppings

· *Slow roast unpeeled garlic cloves and fresh rosemary leaves in olive oil and then squeeze out the garlic flesh and mix with the rosemary and oil.*

· *Cut vine-ripened tomatoes in half and season with chopped garlic, thyme and olive oil.*

· *Slice fennel very finely and mix with lemon thyme and olive oil.*

* If using dried yeast, mix with 75 mL/2¹/2 fl oz of the warm water in a small bowl and leave to activate, 5–8 minutes. If it does not foam, discard and start again with new yeast. Add to the semolina mixture before adding the beer.

** Available from health food shops. Flour packaged as bread flour, hard flour or durum wheat flour is suitable. Do not use bread mix, which is a mix designed for use in bread machines.

1 Place the semolina in a large bowl. Gradually add the water, mixing with a wooden spoon to a porridge consistency. Break up the fresh yeast and mix in by hand. When completely blended, add the beer. When the mixture starts to activate, add the bread flour and the salt. Mix with a wooden spoon initially, then use your hands to form a loose dough. Turn out onto a floured surface and knead until springy and smooth, 8–10 minutes. Rest for 5 minutes.

2 Divide the dough in half. Dust two baking trays liberally with semolina flour. Roll each portion out to a flat oval shape about 2.5 cm/1 in thick and transfer to a prepared tray. Using the tips of your fingers, push holes into the surface. If using a topping such as caramelised garlic or herbs, pat it onto the surface now. Cover with a clean, dry tea towel and allow to prove in a warm, breeze-free spot until almost doubled in size, 1¹/2–2 hours.

3 Preheat the oven to 190°C/375°F/Gas Mark 6. Just before baking drizzle each focaccia with 3 tablespoons of the oil and sprinkle with salt and a little pepper. Transfer to the oven and bake until cooked and golden, 20–25 minutes. Immediately transfer to wire racks to cool.

Smoked beef carpaccio with Mediterranean vegetables and goats cheese

Beef carpaccio is a lovely light way to start a meal. I have smoked the beef in this recipe, which is a different way of incorporating flavour into the meat.

SERVES 6

600 g/1 lb 5 oz centre-cut fillet of beef

Curing mixture
10 black peppercorns
2 tablespoons sea salt
2 teaspoons mixed dried herbs, such
*   as sage, thyme, basil, oregano*
10 juniper berries
1 tablespoon paprika

150 g /5^1/$_2$ oz hickory shavings
100 g/3^1/$_2$ oz dried mushrooms (optional)

Mediterranean vegetables
1 each red, green, yellow capsicum (pepper)
2 teaspoons extra virgin olive oil
1 zucchini (courgette), sliced
1 eggplant (aubergine) weighing about
*   225 g/8 oz each, cut into 1 cm/^{1}/$_2$ in*
*   slices*
salt and freshly ground black pepper
4 semi-dried tomatoes, sliced into strips

❶ Truss the fillet with kitchen twine at 2–3 cm/1 in intervals.

❷ To make the curing mixture, place all the ingredients in a pestle and mortar and crush to a powder. This step can also be done in a spice mill. Rub all over the beef, cover loosely with plastic wrap and refrigerate for 8–10 hours.

❸ Place the hickory shavings in the bottom of a wok and heat over a moderately high heat. Once they start to smoke, add the mushrooms. Position a wire rack or steamer in the wok, place the beef on this and cover with a tight-fitting lid. Reduce the heat to low and smoke for 5 minutes. Do not open the lid. Remove from the heat and rest for 15 minutes to allow the smoke to infuse. Remove the beef and cool.

❹ Grill the capsicums until charred all over. Place in a plastic bag and set aside to cool. Peel off the skin, then cut into slices and dress with half the oil. Grill the zucchini and eggplant and dress with the remaining oil. Season with salt and pepper.

* Available from barbecue suppliers.

Curtis Stone

Dressing

75 g/2¹/₂ oz soft goats cheese, crumbled

2¹/₂ tablespoons tarragon vinegar

2 tablespoons extra virgin olive oil

2 tablespoons peanut (groundnut) oil

salt and freshly ground black pepper

1 cup loosely packed wild rocket

extra goats cheese, for garnish

5 Using a sharp knife, slice the beef as thinly as possible. Fan the slices, overlapping slightly as you go, on a serving plate. Combine the capsicum, zucchini, eggplant and semi-dried tomatoes and place in the centre of the beef.

6 To make the dressing, blend the cheese with the vinegar until smooth. Whisk in the olive oil and peanut oil, and season lightly with salt and pepper. Pour enough over the wild rocket to coat lightly, and place this on top of the vegetables. Drizzle the remaining dressing and crumble a little extra goats cheese over the beef just before serving.

Curtis Stone

Confit tomato tartare with green beans and olives

Confit tomatoes have a lovely intense flavour, which is broken up well by the crunchy green beans.

SERVES 4

6 plum tomatoes
1 tablespoon olive oil
100 g/3¹/₂ oz thin baby green beans
2 garlic cloves, thinly sliced
4 tablespoons extra virgin olive oil
1 tablespoon thyme leaves
1 shallot (eschalot)
1 tablespoon chopped flat leaf parsley
2 teaspoons baby capers
salt and freshly ground black pepper
3 pitted black Spanish olives
1 tablespoon finely chopped chives

❶ Preheat the oven to 110°C/225°F/Gas Mark ¹/₄. Line a baking tray with foil. Bring a large saucepan of water to the boil. Core the tomatoes, cut a cross on the opposite end and plunge into the boiling water for 8–10 seconds. Remove and refresh in iced water, then peel. Add the oil to the saucepan and blanch the beans until just tender, 1–2 minutes. Drain and rinse under very cold water to arrest the cooking. Reserve.

❷ Quarter the tomatoes lengthways and remove the seeds, leaving petal-shaped pieces of flesh. Spread over the prepared tray and place a slice of garlic on each one. Drizzle with 2¹/₂ tablespoons of the extra virgin olive oil and sprinkle the thyme over the top. Place in the oven for 1¹/₂ hours at 80°C/175°F. Cool, then dice and place in a bowl.

❸ Cut the shallot to the same size as the tomatoes and add to the bowl. Add the parsley and capers, and season with salt and pepper. Toss lightly. Place the top (the ring-shaped wall) of a 18 cm/7 in springform tin in the centre of a serving plate and fill with the tartare. Gently lift the ring off leaving a circular mound of tartare.

❹ Slice the olives in half lengthways and place around the tartar. Trim the beans and arrange on top of the tartare in a lattice pattern. Mix the chives with the remaining extra virgin olive oil. Drizzle around the plate and serve.

Curtis Stone

Butternut pumpkin and goats cheese caponata

I read somewhere that caponata in ancient Latin recipes usually involved seafood, but it slowly evolved to using vegetables as economic pressures forced frugality. Caponata generally relies on the balance of a sweet taste with sharp or sour flavours, and this recipe is a perfect combination of the two.

SERVES 4

650 g/1 lb 7 oz butternut pumpkin
    (squash), peeled
2 garlic cloves, thinly sliced
2 dried chillies, crumbled
1 cinnamon stick, broken into slivers
leaves of 1 bunch of sage
200 mL/7 fl oz olive oil
5 tablespoons balsamic vinegar
salt and freshly ground black pepper
2$^{1}/_{2}$ tablespoons sugar
55 g/2 oz fresh goats cheese, crumbled
2 cups loosely packed wild rocket
$^{1}/_{2}$ lemon, quartered

1. Preheat the oven to 160°C/315°F/Gas Mark 3 and line a baking tray with baking paper. Cut the pumpkin into 2.5 cm/1 in slices. Halve these diagonally to give half-moon shapes. Place in a large bowl with the garlic, chilli, cinnamon and sage. Add 1 tablespoon of the oil and 2 tablespoons of the vinegar, and season with salt and pepper. Toss to distribute evenly, then leave for 10 minutes.

2. Spread the pumpkin in a single layer on the prepared baking tray and roast until it is soft and the edges crispy, about 30 minutes. If some is burnt just pick it out.

3. Meanwhile, place the sugar in a small saucepan and melt over a low heat. Continue cooking until it changes to a light gold colour. Remove from the heat and gradually stir in the remaining vinegar. Return to the heat and stir until smooth. Allow to cool.

4. Stir the remaining oil into the vinegar mixture to make a dressing. Toss half with the pumpkin to coat well, then transfer the slices to a large serving plate. Toss the remaining dressing with the rocket. Add a squeeze of lemon. Scatter the goats' cheese over the pumpkin and garnish with the dressed rocket and the lemon wedges.

Wild mushroom risotto

As far as risotto goes my opinion is that anyone who doesn't like it has never eaten one that has been made correctly. If you can get your hands on porcini mushrooms, they are brilliant. The technique used here can be adapted to any kind of risotto you like and because it is an easy thing to cook for a large volume of people, it is a winner for a dinner party.

SERVES 4

750 mL/1¹/₄ pints chicken stock
85 g/3 oz butter
500 g/1 lb 2 oz fresh wild mushrooms, such
    as pine, portabello or porcini, sliced
4 shallots (eschalots), chopped
4 garlic cloves, finely chopped
3 teaspoons chopped thyme
350 g/12 oz aborio rice
200 mL/ 7 fl oz dry white wine
100 g/3¹/₂ oz aged pecorino cheese,
    finely grated
1 tablespoon chopped flat leaf parsley
salt and freshly ground black pepper
extra 15 g/¹/₂ oz aged pecorino cheese,
    shaved, to garnish

1 Put the stock in a saucepan and bring to the boil. Reduce the heat and maintain at a low simmer. Preheat a wide saucepan to a medium head and add one quarter of the butter in a wide saucepan. Add the mushrooms and fry quickly until golden. Remove and reserve. Add half the remaining butter to the pan and lightly fry the shallot, garlic and thyme until softened but not coloured, 1–2 minutes. Add the rice and stir for 1 minute to coat the grains.

2 Add the wine, increase the heat slightly and cook, stirring, until it has almost completely evaporated. Stir in a ladleful of the hot stock, then reduce the heat to medium. Cook, stirring often, until the stock has been absorbed. Add another ladleful of stock, and continue in this way for 10 minutes, then stir through the reserved mushrooms. Continue adding stock until it is all used and the rice is al dente, 8–10 minutes. If the stock runs out before the rice is ready, use hot water. The consistency should be moist but forkable.

3 Remove from the heat, and add the remaining butter, the grated pecorino and the parsley. Season to taste with salt and pepper and stir until the butter melts. Serve, garnished with the pecorino shavings.

Curtis Stone

Vitello tonnato

This is a classic Italian starter usually found in the north. The combination of veal and tuna is delightful. You will need a long sharp knife, as it can be a bit tricky to slice poached meat. The dressing is like a tuna mayonnaise and also works well in salads.

SERVES 4–6

1 kg/2 lb 4 oz piece of veal fillet, trimmed of fat

Dressing
2 free-range egg yolks
juice of 3 lemons
15 capers
1 shallot (eschalot), finely chopped
200 g/7 oz canned tuna in oil, drained
200 mL/7 fl oz peanut (groundnut) oil
about 200 mL/7 fl oz olive oil
salt and freshly ground black pepper

extra capers, to garnish
caper berries, to garnish

❶ Put a large pot of water on to boil. Reduce the heat to a point just below simmering (60°C/140°F). Using a large sheet of plastic wrap, tightly roll up the veal, covering it completely so that it resembles a sausage casing. Twist and knot both ends to seal. Place in the hot water and poach for 1 hour. Check the heat from time to time and maintain it at just below simmering. Remove from the pot, plunge into ice-cold water to stop the cooking process.

❷ To make the dressing, place the egg yolks in a food processor and blend. Add the lemon juice, capers and shallot and process for 1 minute. Add the tuna and process for a further 2 minutes. With the processor still running, gradually add the peanut oil in a steady trickle. Slowly drizzle in the olive oil, tasting as you go (depending on the strength of the olive oil, the flavour may become a little too powerful). If the dressing becomes too thick, add a little hot water. Pass through a fine sieve and season to taste with salt and pepper.

❸ To serve, spread a circle of dressing over the centre of a serving platter. Remove the veal from the plastic wrap and slice thinly. Arrange the slices in a fan over the dressing and garnish with capers and caper berries.

Curtis Stone

Roast leg of lamb wrapped in rosemary

There is really nothing like the flavour of this dish: the way the rosemary penetrates the meat with its flavour and the resulting pan juices is awesome. Don't skimp on the rosemary. A top tip to check that roasted lamb is cooked is to take a knife and make an incision like a pocket in the length of the leg bone towards the shank. Place one or two fingers in the incision and if the meat feels warm to hot it is cooked.

SERVES 4–6

*1 leg of lamb, hip joint removed
(sometimes sold as Ezicarve),
weighing about 2 kg/4¹/₂ lb
4 garlic cloves, cut into slivers
6 anchovy fillets, quartered
freshly ground black pepper
2 tablespoons olive oil
10–12 branches of rosemary
100 g/3¹/₂ oz black olive paste*
juice of ¹/₂ lemon*

1 Dry the lamb well and hang or rest in a cool, dry spot until its surface is dry to the touch. This makes all the difference to the flavour. Trim off and discard any excess fat. Make incisions all over the meat using a small sharp knife, creating small pockets about knuckle deep. Stuff a garlic sliver and a piece of anchovy into each incision, then season the surface well with pepper.

2 Heat half the oil in a flameproof heavy-duty baking pan and brown the lamb on all sides over a medium/high heat. Allow to cool.

3 Preheat the oven to 200°C/400°F/Gas Mark 7. Stretch a good length of kitchen string along the work surface and overlap the branches of rosemary along the length of the string. Smear the lamb with the olive paste and place it on the rosemary at one end. Roll it up so that it's completely encased in the rosemary and tie the string tightly to secure. It doesn't matter how crudely you do this — as long as the rosemary stays in place.

continued over...

4 Return the lamb to the baking pan, drizzle with the remaining oil and the lemon juice and place in the oven. Roast for 15 minutes per 500 g/ 1 lb 2 oz, plus 15 minutes more, turning occasionally to cook evenly. Remove from the oven and rest the meat for one-third of the time it took to cook. This ensures a perfectly pink result. Reserve the rosemary for garnish, carve and serve.

* Where black olive paste is unavailable, use 100 g/3½ oz pitted kalamata olives and purée.

Ben O'Donoghue

Fresh fig, honey and rosemary calzone

This is one of those odd Italian combinations that was shown to me by an Italian chef friend in London. He used grapes, but this combination works just as well.

MAKES 8 INDIVIDUAL CALZONE

½ batch Focaccia dough (see page 121)
or use 500 g/1 lb 2 oz block
of puff pastry
6 ripe figs
4 tablespoons mascarpone
4 tablespoons olive oil
2 tablespoons honey
½ tablespoon chopped rosemary
olive oil, for brushing
8 sprigs of rosemary
icing sugar, for dusting
cinnamon, for dusting

1. Place the dough in an oiled bowl and cover with plastic wrap. Leave in a warm spot until doubled in size, about 1½ hours.

2. Preheat the oven to hot 200°C/400°F/Gas Mark 7 and line two baking trays with baking paper. Knock the dough down and divide into eight equal balls. Roll each out on a well-floured work surface to an 8–10 cm/3–4 in circle 3 mm/⅛ in thick.

3. Discard the figs' stalks and slice them into four wedges. Place the wedges side by side along the centre of each circle of dough. Add a teaspoon of mascarpone and a teaspoon of olive oil, then drizzle with a little honey and sprinkle some chopped rosemary over the top. Brush the rims of the circles with additional oil. Fold half of the dough over the top of the figs to encase them, forming a half moon shape. Press the rims of dough together to seal, and crimp the edges.

4. Place on the prepared baking trays, ensuring they are well spaced. Brush with more oil, drizzle with a little extra honey and place a sprig of rosemary on top of each. Bake for 15–20 minutes, or until crisp and golden. Immediately transfer to wire racks to cool. Serve warm, dusted with icing sugar and a sprinkling of cinnamon. Delicious with vanilla ice-cream.

Orange granita with mascarpone

I always say that you should eat for the season and climate. On a hot summer's day you need something refreshing, so a granita is perfect. You can make granita from almost anything — from fruit juices to champagne. They are a great palate cleanser, so may be served between courses.

SERVES 4

about 800 mL/1^1/$_2$ pt water
300 g/11 oz caster sugar
finely grated zest of 2 small oranges
250 mL/9 fl oz orange juice, chilled
2^1/$_2$ tablespoons lemon juice
3 additional oranges
75 mL/2^1/$_2$ fl oz Muscat
250 g/9 oz mascarpone cheese

1. Place 50 mL/2 fl oz of the water in a saucepan with 2^1/$_2$ tablespoons of the sugar. Add the zest and bring slowly to the boil. Remove from heat, and strain into a bowl. Stir in the orange and lemon juice, and place in the freezer. Once ice crystals start to form — in about 15–20 minutes — stir the mixture with a fork to break them up. Return to the freezer and continue this procedure until the mixture resembles snow.

2. Using a sharp knife or a vegetable peeler, thinly peel the other oranges, ensuring that no pith is left on the peel. Slice it into thin strips. Cover with cold water and bring to the boil. Strain, then return to the empty saucepan and add 250 mL/ 9 fl oz water and the remaining sugar. Slowly bring to the boil, then reduce head to a simmer over a very low heat for 1^1/$_2$–2 hours.

3. Mix the Muscat into the mascarpone cheese and place in the bottom of four dessert glasses. Place a large spoonful of granita on top, and garnish with the confit orange zest.

Curtis Stone

Tasmania

Tasmania

Strahan, Wild Salmon and Gruff

Tasmania has a rich and unique history and where once its economy was based on mining, agriculture and primary resources, today eco-tourism and the production of gourmet food products are the key ingredients to Tasmania's success.

The thing I noticed about Tasmania the first time I went there was the weather. It's milder than the mainland and the island climate ensures that the varied localised weather systems keep the island green and clean. Every time I've been, it's been sunny and beautiful. Interestingly, Hobart is statistically the second driest city in Australia, yet close by there is an abundance of temperate rainforest, mountainscapes where snow falls, and thick dense forests. Hobart is also the second oldest Australian capital city. Settlers and convicts first came to what was then called Van Diemen's Land in 1803. Convicts continued to be transported there from England, often for petty crimes, until 1853. They played a major part in the colony's early development providing labour and skills, such as building and architecture. The convicts and their warders added a dark side to the history of the island, with foreboding places like Port Arthur and the entrance to Macquarie Harbour in Strahan known as 'Hell's Gates'. A prison sentence in Tasmania struck fear into many hearts.

Strahan, where we spent most of our time, is located in a natural amphitheatre overlooking the vast, protected Macquarie Harbour, a safe anchorage on the notorious and rugged west coast. There's nothing to stop the waves of the Roaring Forties between here and South Africa. Macquarie Harbour is almost 80 square nautical miles, which is almost six times the size of Sydney Harbour.

There's an amusing story of a group of convicts in Strahan who, after building a sailing ship under the watchful eyes of their guards, stole the ship in the middle of the night and sailed it

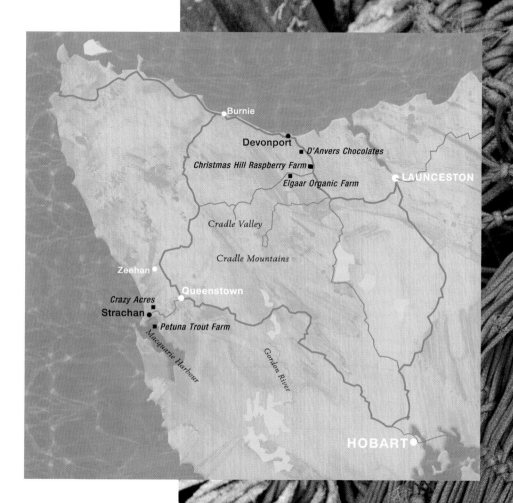

Burnie

Devonport
■ D'Anvers Chocolates
Christmas Hill Raspberry Farm ■
■ Elgaar Organic Farm

LAUNCESTON

Cradle Valley

Cradle Mountains

Zeehan

Queenstown

Crazy Acres ■
Strachan ●
■ Petuna Trout Farm

Macquarie Harbour

Gordon River

HOBART ●

to South America. Remarkably they made it, but were recaptured and extradited to England to stand trial. At the trial it came to light that because the ship had yet to be commissioned it could not therefore be classed as a ship, so the convicts had their charges altered to 'stealing lumber'. Their punishment was to be transported back to Strahan to, I presume, build more ships. I find it amazing that Prisoners of Her Majesty (POHMs) were sent to a place like Strahan, which to me looks more like paradise than hell — it is picture postcard stuff.

Many tourists flock to Strahan to experience its unhurried pace and to experience the magnificent World Heritage Area of the Gordon River and the ancient Huon pine forests.

Tasmania's building heritage is well preserved and the landscape is dotted with European-inspired sandstone and brick buildings in abundance. With the predominant colour being green, these buildings give the international visitor the impression that they haven't left Europe at all. Driving through some towns felt just like being in Devon or Wales.

Apart from the history there were two other reasons to include Tasmania on our itinerary. First, since we'd been away, this tiny island had been developing an incredible reputation for first-class food and agricultural produce. Whereas once Tassie evoked images of apples and more bloody apples, today it's Pinot Noir, smoked salmon, lobsters, ocean trout, wild berries, truffles, matured cheeses, Brie and much more. The second reason was to meet up with a long-time mate of mine Steve (whom we call Herb, so we don't get him mixed up with his dad), and Herb's dad (also Steve, obviously), whom everyone calls Gruff. Gruff lives on an 8-hectare (20-acre) property called Crazy Acres, just outside Strahan. Gruff loves a drink, listening to a yarn, AC/DC and C & W, and fishing. He's a kind of Aussie Osborne, a real character, and so are all his mates.

Let's start at the beginning of this journey. We drove the jeep onto the trans-Tasman ferry in Melbourne, wandered upstairs to put our gear into the cabin, then settled down at the bar to have a drink or two and a chat with some fellow travellers. The new car ferry is quite popular. After leaving port at around nine in the evening, we arrived in Devonport at six in the morning, feeling refreshed after a good night's sleep. Herb was waiting for us in Strahan and, so as not to arrive empty-handed, we headed out to search for some local delicacies.

A short drive along the highway from Devonport we called in at D'Anvers chocolates. (D'Anvers means 'from Antwerp', I'm told.) Curtis and I believe that anytime is the right time for good chocolate and so we headed in. There we met Igor Van Gerwen, a Belgium-born and trained chocolatier who now calls Tasmania home. He invited us into his kitchen — there is nothing better than the smell of warm chocolate. D'Anvers makes everything by hand and so their maximum output is just 1000 kilograms (about 2200 pounds) per week.

Some of Igor's staff were piping traditional truffles, then coating them in dark chocolate and rolling them in shaved almonds. They let us have a go ourselves. Luckily part of a chef's training is piping all sorts of things, so we soon got the hang of it. The chocolate also inspired Curtis and he took some white couverture chocolate with him.

The basic difference between couverture chocolate (the kind Igor uses) and compound chocolate (the kind you buy in block form) is twofold. The first is that couverture chocolate is made with a relatively expensive ingredient, cocoa butter. Compound chocolate uses animal fat or vegetable margarine instead. That's what can leave the slightly greasy texture in the mouth. The second difference is that compound chocolate has a fineness of 30 to 35 microns, while Igor's couverture chocolate is 10 to 12 microns. In other words, it's three times finer. This means it's smoother on the palate and simply melts away on the tongue, leaving just a rich chocolate taste to savour.

Just a little further on we saw a roadside sign for fresh raspberries and stopped in at the Christmas Hill Raspberry Farm. Lindi Dourauf took us down past the lake to where the raspberries grow in rows on the hillside. Lindi has twelve different varieties planted over 4 hectares (10 acres), which are all picked by hand. The raspberries are available fresh from late summer through autumn and snap frozen the rest of the year. I couldn't pick the subtle differences between the varieties, even with careful sampling during the Ben-style picking: one for me, one for the bucket …

We next tracked down Joe and Antonia Gretschmann at Elgaar Organic Farm. Although the Gretschmanns have been in Australia for two decades, their family has been making cheeses in Germany since the 1450s. Their farm is completely organic and built according to time-honoured plans. The cellars, for example, are built of stone and are completely underground in the Bavarian style. The temperature in there is cool, even slightly cold, which is achieved without any air-conditioning or cooling. I was impressed by how simply things worked: where the sun hits the building, the cellar is dry; on the other side, the cellar is moist.

The cheeses are part-made in an impressive Swiss copper vat that shines brightly as the result of liberally applied elbow grease. As in Europe, the cellars have their own natural flora and no foreign starter cultures need to be introduced. The Gretschmanns make their own starter culture in a method that has been handed down for generations. This fascinated us but despite numerous attempts, we were unable to get even a hint of how it is done. Many Elgaar cheeses are supplied to restaurants on the mainland. They are stored at the farm until they are needed and on request are freighted one by one. And it is not just fabulous cheeses that the Gretschmanns produce. They also produce milk (in bottles, no less), yoghurt, mascarpone, and cultured, unsalted butter in a traditional wooden German churn.

Our next stop was to Petuna Seafoods ocean trout farm located in the perfectly pristine Macquarie Harbour, a short boat-ride from Strahan and on the edge of the World Heritage Wilderness Area. The scenery is breathtaking. Strahan harbour is perfect for farming ocean trout because the fish require both fresh and salt water to thrive. In this unique place, fresh water flows in a top layer from the famous Franklin and Gordon rivers, while salt water from the Southern Ocean flows a little deeper through the massive pens. Another reason this environment is so perfect is that the naturally stained waters of the harbour protect the fish from sunburn!

The trout are reared from the beginning in hatcheries in the north of Tasmania and then, after about twelve months, they are transferred to the pens in Macquarie Harbour. The fish grow to about 2–4 kilograms (4–8 pounds) before they are harvested. Each pen holds approximately 7000 fish and 1500 tonnes (over 3000 pounds) of ocean trout and Atlantic salmon are harvested each year. That's a heck of a lot of sushi!

When we eventually made it to Strahan, through some of the most beautiful countryside in the world, what we really needed was a cleansing ale with Herb and Gruff. The boys didn't let us down. Strahan was once a sleepy little spot on the map, but today it's a vibrant village with tourists and locals flocking to mix in the local café and waterfront pub. I have always loved coming to Tassie. It's a big-hearted place full of real people in a genuinely beautiful part of the world. No wonder I keep coming back.

Pink-eye potato, olive and caper salad

I love these potatoes. They're so full of flavour, and their waxy yellow colour makes the best potato salad you will come across. If you can't get them use a pink fir apple potato or a kipfler potato, both of which have a similarly pleasant flavour and texture.

SERVES 4–6

1 kg/2 lb 4 oz pink-eye (pink fir) potatoes
$^1/_2$ garlic clove
salt
2 tablespoons coarsely chopped flat leaf
    parsley
100 g/3$^1/_2$ oz baby capers (if salted, soak
    in cold water for 30 minutes and
    rinse well)
200 g/7 oz pitted large green olives
2 tablespoons white wine vinegar
100 mL/3$^1/_2$ fl oz extra virgin olive oil
freshly ground black pepper
finely peeled zest of 1 lemon
2 tablespoons white celery leaves

1. Place the potatoes in a large saucepan and cover with cold water. Add salt, bring to the boil and simmer until tender, about 20 minutes, depending on size. In a large mortar, smash the garlic with a little salt, then add half the parsley and roughly smash. Add the capers and olives and do the same to give a coarse, roughly broken up texture.

2. Peel and cut the potatoes in half while still hot. Add the vinegar and oil. Cool for 10 minutes, then add the olive and parsley mixture. Season with salt and pepper, and toss through the zest, celery leaves and remaining parsley.

3. Great served with fish or poached chicken.

Ben O'Donoghue

Smoked salmon with fennel and dill salad

I find when you are serving seafood it is very nice to break up the texture with something crisp or crunchy. The fennel and dill salad is actually like a pickle so it remains very crunchy and fresh, which cuts through the richness of the salmon.

SERVES 4

2 baby fennel bulbs, trimmed
100 g/3¹/₂ oz coarse rock salt
300 mL/10¹/₂ fl oz water
200 g/7 oz caster sugar
5 tablespoons white wine vinegar
¹/₂ cup finely chopped dill
5 tablespoons extra virgin olive oil
1 tablespoon lemon juice
salt and freshly ground black pepper
200 g/7 oz sliced smoked salmon

1 Slice the fennel bulb on a mandolin or using the thinnest blade on a food processor to give slices that are almost transparent. Place in a bowl and toss with the salt. Set aside for 10 minutes. Place the water, sugar and vinegar in a saucepan and bring to just below boiling. Remove from the heat. Wash the salt from the fennel under running water. Place the fennel in a clean bowl and pour the vinegar mixture over the top. Cover and set aside for 12 hours.

2 Mix half the dill through the fennel. Combine the remaining dill with the oil and lemon juice. Season with salt and pepper. Arrange the smoked salmon around the edge of a serving platter. Squeeze the excess liquid from the fennel and pile it in the centre of the platter. Sprinkle with more pepper and drizzle the dill dressing around the outside of the platter.

Curtis Stone

Stuffed zucchini-flower fritters with wild rocket pesto

Anyone who has ever had a vegetable garden will know that on the end of a zucchini (courgette) grows a small flower. These flowers have a taste similar to the zucchini but a little milder. The nature of the flower enables us to stuff them with all sorts of flavoursome ingredients.

If your local greengrocer doesn't stock them ask for some to be ordered for you, once you start to demand them they will supply them.

SERVES 4

150 g/5 ¹/₂ oz ricotta cheese
¹/₂ teaspoon lemon juice
4 basil leaves, shredded
55 g/2 oz freshly grated Parmesan cheese
salt and freshly ground black pepper
12 zucchini (courgette) flowers

Batter
100 g/3¹/₂ oz plain flour
125 mL/4¹/₂ fl oz soda water

vegetable oil, for deep-frying
seasoned plain flour, for dusting
¹/₂ cup loosely packed basil leaves
30 g/1 oz freshly grated Parmesan
   cheese, for serving

1. Mix the ricotta, lemon juice, basil and Parmesan together, and season with salt and pepper. Cut the stalks off the zucchini flowers, leaving 1 cm/¹/₂ in attached. Slice the stalks in half lengthways. Open a flower and spoon cheese mixture (1–2 teaspoons, depending on the size of the flowers), into the cavity to two-thirds full. Twist the end of the petals to close up. Repeat with the remaining filling and flowers.

2. To make the batter, mix the flour and soda water with a spoon until smooth.

3. Fill a large pan with vegetable oil to a depth of 10 cm/4 in and heat. When hot, dust the stuffed flowers and stalks with the seasoned flower. Dip into the batter and fry in batches until golden brown. Remove from the oil and place on paper towels to drain. Deep-fry the basil leaves.

4. Sprinkle the flowers and stalks with the Parmesan and serve at once, topped with the fried basil leaves and accompanied by wild rocket pesto.

continued over...

Curtis Stone

Wild rocket pesto

100 g/3½ oz toasted pine nuts
85 g/3 oz freshly grated Parmesan
*   cheese*
1 garlic clove, crushed
1 cup loosely packed wild rocket leaves
1 cup loosely packed flat leaf parsley
1 teaspoon lemon juice
2½ tablespoons extra virgin olive oil
salt and freshly ground black pepper

1 Place the pine nuts, Parmesan, garlic, rocket and parsley in a food processor. Pulse until fine. Add the lemon juice and pulse to blend.

2 With the motor running, gradually add the olive oil in a trickle. Season with salt and pepper.

Curtis Stone

Salt-baked onion with truffled egg

In Tasmania's cooler climate the vegetables grow more slowly and therefore have a greater intensity of flavour. The root vegies, especially, benefit from this climate. Having heard that they were growing truffles here I thought the combination of flavours in this recipe would be quite exciting. If fresh truffles prove too expensive, then truffle oil works really well — just don't use too much. This dish is a real winter warmer.

SERVES 4

1 kg/2 lb 4 oz rock salt

4 large organic brown onions

4 sprigs of rosemary

2 teaspoons butter

1 garlic clove, crushed

250 mL/9 fl oz pouring cream

100 g/3$^{1}/_{2}$ oz Taleggio cheese, cubed

salt and freshly ground black pepper

4 free-range egg yolks

$^{1}/_{2}$ teaspoon truffle oil

55 g/2 oz Parmesan cheese, freshly grated

1 Preheat the oven to 150°C/300°F/Gas Mark 3. Spread the salt over the bottom of a baking tray. Leaving the onions unpeeled, prick a hole in the top of each with a small knife and push in a sprig of rosemary. Transfer to the salt on the prepared tray and bake until soft, about 1 hour.

2 Remove from the oven and lift the onions off the salt. Allow to cool for 10 minutes. Slice the top quarter off each onion and reserve for a lid. Scoop out and reserve each onion centre leaving a thin (1–2 layers) outer shell. Roughly mince the reserved onion.

3 Melt the butter in a pan and gently cook the minced onion and garlic until sweet and golden brown, 8–10 minutes. Add the cream and reduce by half. Remove from the heat and add the Taleggio cheese. Stir until melted and season to taste with salt and pepper. Return the onion shells to the salted tray and half fill them with the creamed onion. Gently place an egg yolk on top, and sprinkle each with 2–3 drops of oil. Top with the remaining creamed onion mixture. Sprinkle with the Parmesan cheese, return to the oven and bake until golden, about 10 minutes. Serve with a salad of bitter salad leaves dressed with balsamic vinegar.

Ben O'Donoghue

Rock oysters Florentine

Oysters cook very quickly, so need only a little time under the grill. The lovely velvety consistency of the Hollandaise sauce makes this a luxurious dish.

SERVES 4

24 rock oysters (any oysters will do),
    freshly shucked
1.5 kg/3 lb 5 oz rock salt
2 teaspoons butter
200 g/7 oz picked baby spinach leaves
salt and freshly ground pepper
150 mL/5½ fl oz hollandaise sauce
    (see page 47 and make the Béarnaise
    sauce, leaving out the tarragon leaves)
24 sprigs of chervil, to garnish

1. Remove the oysters from their shells and place in a saucepan with their juices. Clean and dry the shells. Spread the rock salt over an oven tray and place the oyster shells on top.

2. Heat the butter in a saucepan, add the spinach and fry until just wilted. Transfer to a clean tea towel and squeeze out excess moisture. Season lightly with salt and pepper. Place a small amount into each oyster shell.

3. Preheat the grill to hot. Warm the oysters and their juices quickly over a moderate heat. Return them to their shell, on top of the spinach. Spoon 1½ teaspoons hollandaise sauce over each oyster. Place the oven tray under the grill and cook until the sauce on the oysters is hot and golden. Garnish with the chervil and serve at once.

Curtis Stone

Warm salad of grilled smoked eel

I absolutely love smoked eel, its rich oiliness is fantastic set against the sharp crispiness of this salad. It's a fantastic, light way to start a meal. If these devilish little creatures aren't your cup of tea then use smoked trout or smoked salmon; just don't grill the stuff. Serve them cold as their textures are less firm and not suitable for grilling.

SERVES 4

1 large fennel bulb
1 medium red onion
^{1}/$_2$ radicchio head
1 cup lightly packed flat leaf parsley
1 cup loosely packed sorrel leaves
300 g/11 oz smoked eel, skinned
    and boned
1^1/$_2$ tablespoons extra virgin olive oil
salt and freshly ground black pepper
1 lemon, halved

❶ Trim the fennel, reserving the green tops. Slice thinly across the bulb and place in iced water to crisp up. Halve the onion lengthways, and slice lengthways. Place in a bowl. Separate the radicchio leaves and tear into small pieces, discarding the white centre of each leaf. Add the radicchio, parsley and sorrel to the onion.

❷ Cut the smoked eel into four equal fillets and brush with a little oil. Heat a griddle pan to high and sear the eel on both sides, 2–3 minutes.

❸ Meanwhile, drain the fennel and add to the onion and radicchio. Season to taste with salt and pepper, and add the remaining oil and the juice of half the lemon. Break up the reserved fennel tops and add to the salad. Toss gently.

❹ Remove the eel from the pan and squeeze a little lemon over the top. Crumble into the salad and serve.

Ben O'Donoghue

Salt-baked ocean trout

Fantastic for a summer lunch or dinner.

SERVES 10

1 kg/2 lb 4 oz cheap black olives
5 kg/11 lb rock salt*
2 egg whites, lightly whisked
2 kg/4¹/₂ lb whole ocean trout (freshly
    gutted, and with the gills removed)**
1 bunch of rosemary
2 lemons, sliced

❶ To prepare the salt crust, place the olives in a food processor, stones and all, and pulse to chop them. Transfer to a large bowl, then add the salt and egg white. Mix well.

❷ On a baking tray large enough to hold the trout, using half of the salt, make a bed 2–3 cm/1 in thick in the shape of the fish. Place the trout on top. Stuff the rosemary and lemon slices into the cavity of the fish to prevent the salt from getting in and making it overly salty.

❸ Preheat the oven to 180°C/350°F/Gas Mark 5. Cover the fish with the remaining salt to a thickness similar to the bottom. If need be, use scrunched up aluminium foil to make a retaining wall around the outside to hold the salt in place. Place in the oven and bake for 20 minutes. Remove from the oven and check that the fish is cooked by placing a small knife or roasting fork into the thickest part. Touch it to your lips and if it's warm, the fish is done. Allow to rest for 10 minutes before removing the crust.

❹ Using a serrated knife, saw around the base, being careful not to cut into the flesh of the fish. Lift the top off; it may come away in one piece or break into several pieces. Brush any excess salt off the fish with a wet pastry brush.

❺ To serve, peel back the skin and cut down the centre of the fish, removing the flesh in portions. It should be wonderfully moist and pink

* It might be less expensive to buy this quantity of rock salt from a hardware shop or pool shop.
** If your oven is a standard domestic one, buy two whole ocean trout about 1.4 kg/3 lb in size, and use two baking trays. There will be enough salt crust to cover both.

Veal escalopes with wild mushrooms, mozzarella and Madeira sauce

Veal is a lovely meat that cooks very quickly. If you overcook veal, it can get quite dry. By serving mozzarella and pasta with the veal escalopes you end up with a lovely moist dish.

SERVES 4

Tomato fondue
6–8 large ripe plum tomatoes
2 teaspoons extra virgin olive oil
1 small shallot (eschalot), finely chopped
1 garlic clove, finely chopped
1 fresh bay leaf
1 sprig of thyme

2 tablespoons olive oil
1 shallot (eschalot), finely chopped
1 garlic clove, finely chopped
200 g/7 oz mixed wild mushrooms
    (portobello, Swiss brown, chantarelles,
    pine), sliced
salt and freshly ground black pepper
3/4 cup chopped flat leaf parsley
300 g/11 oz fresh tagliatelle
1 teaspoon warm water
4 x 120 g/4 oz escalopes of veal cut
    from the loin
1 ball of buffalo mozzarella, cut into
    8 slices

1. To make the tomato fondue, core the tomatoes and slice a cross in their tops. Plunge into a pan of boiling water for 12–15 seconds. Peel and dice when cool enough to handle.

2. Heat the oil in a saucepan and add the shallot and garlic. Fry, without colouring, over a low heat for 2–3 minutes. Add the tomato, bay leaf and thyme. Partially cover and cook, stirring often, over a low heat for 2–2$\frac{1}{2}$ hours, or until it becomes dry and thick. Push through a sieve into a smaller saucepan and keep warm.

3. Heat 2 teaspoons of oil in a medium frying pan and add the shallot and garlic. Fry, without browning, for 1 minute. Increase the heat and add the mushrooms. Cook, stirring, for 1$\frac{1}{2}$–2 minutes. Season with salt and pepper, and add half the parsley. Keep warm.

4. Meanwhile, bring a large pot of water to the boil. Add the tagliatelle and cook until al dente. Drain. Place in a bowl with 2 teaspoons of oil and the water. Season with salt and pepper, and sprinkle with the remaining parsley.

continued over...

Curtis Stone

⑤ Heat the remaining oil in a large frying pan. Season the veal, fry in batches over a moderately high heat for 1 minute each side. Remove from the pan and spread one side with a little tomato fondue.

⑥ Preheat the grill to hot. Arrange two slices of mozzarella over the tomato fondue on each escalope. Place under the grill for 10 seconds, or until the cheese is soft.

⑦ To serve, pile a quarter of the tagliatelle in the centre of each of four serving plates. Place the veal on the pasta, and spoon the wild mushrooms around the outside of each plate. Garnish with the remaining tomato fondue, and drizzle with Madeira sauce.

Madeira sauce

1 tablespoon olive oil
100 g/3¹/₂ oz veal trimmings
*   (available from butcher)*
2 shallots (eschalots), finely sliced
2 garlic cloves, crushed
55 g/2 oz mushrooms, sliced
1 sprig of thyme
3 fresh bay leaves
5 white peppercorns
1 tablespoon sherry vinegar
1 tablespoon cognac
300 mL/10¹/₂ fl oz Madeira
300 mL/10¹/₂ fl oz veal stock
2¹/₂ tablespoons water

① Heat the oil in a large frying pan and fry the veal until golden brown. Add the shallot, garlic, mushrooms, thyme, bay leaves and peppercorns and cook over a moderate heat for 5 minutes, stirring often. Add the sherry vinegar and cook until all the liquid has evaporated. Add the cognac and stir to deglaze the pan.

② Pour in the Madeira and simmer until reduced by two-thirds, 12–15 minutes. Add the stock and water, and bring to the boil. Simmer for 20 minutes, removing any scum that may develop. Pass through a fine sieve into a small saucepan and keep warm.

Curtis Stone

Raspberry and almond tart

Raspberries rock. Here their sharp berry flavour contrasts with the crumbly sweet pastry and the nutty, buttery flavour of the frangipane filling. Serve with double cream for a sensual touch to a classic tart. Wicked!

SERVES 8–10

Pastry

335 g/11¹/₂ oz plain flour
100 g/3¹/₂ oz icing sugar
235 g/8¹/₂ oz unsalted butter, cubed
3 free-range egg yolks

Filling

250 g/9 oz unsalted butter, cubed
250 g/9 oz caster sugar
1 vanilla pod, split in half lengthways
250 g/9 oz ground almonds
pinch salt

750 g/1 lb 10 oz fresh raspberries
icing sugar, to serve

1. To make the pastry, place the flour, sugar and butter in a food processor, and blend to a fine breadcrumb texture. Add the egg yolks, one at a time, and mix until the dough just comes together. Wrap in plastic wrap and freeze for half an hour.

2. To make the filling, combine the butter and sugar in a food processor to give a soft but not overly whipped mixture. Scrape in the seeds from the vanilla pod and add the almond meal and salt. Mix thoroughly.

3. Grease a 28 cm/11 in fluted loose-bottomed tart tin. Grate half of the pastry into the prepared tin. Using the tips of your fingers, press the pastry over the base. Grate the remaining pastry in and press into the edges of the tin, to the same thickness as the bottom. Rest in the refridgerator for at least 30 minutes.

4. Preheat the oven to 190°C/375°F/Gas Mark 6. Bake the tart case, uncovered, for 15 minutes. Set aside to cool. Reduce the oven temperature to 180°C/350°/Gas Mark 5. Scatter one-third of the raspberries over the bottom of the tart case then spoon the almond mix over the top. Bake for 30 minutes, or until just firm and golden brown. Allow to cool.

5. To serve, push indentations all over the surface with your fingertips, and fill with the rest of the raspberries. Slice and dust with icing sugar.

Lemon creams with poached cherries

Tasmanian dairy produce is just about the best you can get anywhere in the world, so why come all this way and not take advantage of it? This dessert is a bit of a calorie killer but hey, what the hell. It's dead easy, but you'll need a thermometer. Use two lemons if you like a subtle lemon flavour, or three for more of a zing. I like using frozen sour cherries to cook with — fresh cherries should be eaten fresh.

SERVES 6

875 mL/1¹/₂ pt double/thick cream (35 per cent fat content)
finely grated zest and juice of 2–3 lemons
170 g/6 oz caster sugar

Poached cherries
finely grated zest of ¹/₂ orange
200 mL/7 fl oz red wine (Shiraz or Cabernet Sauvignon)
¹/₂ stick of cinnamon
1 clove
1 teaspoon caster sugar, plus extra, if needed
200 g/7 oz frozen black sour cherries, defrosted

1 In a saucepan, heat the cream to 75°C/165°F. Remove from the heat and cool to 65°C/150°F.

2 Add the lemon zest, juice and sugar to the cream mixture and mix well. Allow to cool, then pour into six ³/₄-cup capacity moulds (cups or glasses will do if you don't have moulds*). Place on a tray and put in the refrigerator to set, about 4 hours.

3 When ready to serve, carefully up-end the moulds over serving plates and give them a shake; the creams should just slip out. If this proves difficult, run a small knife around the edge of the mould to release the cream and try again. Serve with poached cherries.

4 To poach the cherries: place the zest, wine, cinnamon, clove and sugar in a saucepan, and bring to a simmer. Add the cherries, bring to the boil, and taste for sweetness. If necessary, add a little more sugar to neutralise the tannin of the wine, but retaining some zing. Simmer for 5 minutes, then cool.

5 Serve each lemon cream accompanied by 5–6 cherries. Drizzle a little of the syrup over each one.

You can also make moulds from 60 mm/3 in diameter PVC pipe from a hardware shop cut to depths of 30 mm/1¹/₄ in. Sand the edges and then seal the bottoms with plastic cling wrap.

Frozen berries with hot white chocolate sauce

I would usually advise people not to use frozen berries; however, with this chocolate sauce, the second the hot sauce and the frozen berries touch, the sauce solidifies making a lovely mound of chocolate-covered berries. The heat from the sauce also begins to break down the berries. It's hard to describe in words, but believe me it's worth trying.

SERVES 4

150 g/5^1/$_2$ oz fresh raspberries
150 g/5^1/$_2$ oz fresh blue berries
150 g/5^1/$_2$ oz fresh blackberries
250 mL/9 fl oz pouring cream
2 vanilla pods, split in half lengthways
250 g/9 oz white chocolate,
    finely chopped

1 Spread the berries on a tray, making sure they are well spaced. Cover with plastic wrap and transfer to the freezer. Leave until frozen.

2 Place the cream and vanilla pods in a saucepan and heat to just below simmering. Place the chocolate in a bowl and strain the cream over the chocolate. Stir constantly until smooth.

3 Arrange the berries on a serving platter and pour the hot sauce over the top. Serve at once.

Curtis Stone

Margaret River

Margaret River

Wino's, Waves and Chardonnays

Ben O'Donoghue

Curtis and I lobbed into Perth, Western Australia, direct from London, bleary-eyed and jet-lagged. We're here because this is where I did most of my growing up. We're also here to check out what's been happening in the food scene. And to squeeze in a surf or two, something I don't get the chance to do as often as I'd like in Old Blighty. With this in mind, it made sense that we should drive straight to Margaret River, about three and a half hours south of Perth, famous (even in London) for its award-winning wines, gourmet foods, brilliant coastline, forests and spectacular (although sometimes downright bloody dangerous) surf beaches.

The Margaret River region has had an interesting history, starting over a century ago producing timber. The massive karri and tuart hardwoods soar more than 60 metres (200 feet) into the sky, their gun-barrel-straight trunks were ideal for, among other things, the masts of giant sailing ships. In the early 1900s, logging and clearing had transformed a lot of the land from lush forest to dairy country. Beef farming followed shortly after. Today Margaret River is probably best known for its international award-winning wine industry which, surprisingly, did not start out until the early 1970s, making the winemakers' achievements even greater. Apparently, an agricultural scientist working for the State government researched the area and discovered that it had an almost identical micro-culture to the famous French wine-producing region of Bordeaux, so I guess it was inevitable that, unrestrained by centuries of unchanging and legislated techniques, it would end up rivalling them. I even have some Margaret River wines on the wine list in my restaurant. As well as being good wines, they remind me of home.

After the road trip from Perth, which passed without incident (except for a speeding ticket!), we drove along the main street of Margaret River and decided to head for the 'main break', where the river meets the sea. When we parked, the swell and the wind weren't working for us, so we headed a couple of ks south to a spot I knew as 'Grunters'. Just as we got there a whole busload of schoolkids arrived for their weekly surf lesson, so the traffic on the break was a little

Donnybrook

Dunsborough

Yallingup

Busselton

Venison Farm ■

Howard Park
Vasse Felix ■■ ■ Madfish Bay Winery
Gracetown ● ■ Olio Bello

Nannup

● Margaret River

Caves Rd

Karridale ● ■ *Cloverdene*

● Augusta

like the Kings Road, Chelsea, on a Saturday morning. It's not good for the ego to get shown up by a bunch of pimply, pre-pubescent twelve-year-olds carving up the waves. We decided to go elsewhere.

From the cliff top we could see a nice break a little further south. There were only a few guys out, so we headed down. Curtis has got this 'Noah' (Noah's Ark= shark) phobia, so I dreamed up some stories about mates who'd been taken from this exact spot. He waxed the board for a little longer than normal while he slyly checked the waves for fins. A big pod of dolphins breaking the surface out the back of the waves made him look twice.

We pulled on our wetties, strapped on the leggies and paddled out. Out the back of the breakers we said g'day to the other crew. Amazingly, among them was a bloke named Aaron Carr, whom I had done my apprenticeship with. I knew he was down this way and was hoping to catch up. Knowing Aaron, the first place I should have thought to look was the surf. (If you think this sounds like a bit too much of a coincidence, we encountered an even better one. Later that day, Curtis called his brother Luke — who lives in Melbourne and whom he hasn't seen for three years — and when Curtis asked where he was, he said Margaret River. Unbelievably, Luke was a couple of ks away with his girlfriend.)

Anyway, as there's a fair bit of sitting around and waiting when you surf, we got to talking to these guys and found they were all mostly in the food or wine business. It seems most of them are there for the surf first and the job second. Curtis and I said that if they scored us some produce, we'd knock up a meal. Aaron, who's head chef at Vasse Felix winery, said we could use his kitchen.

One of the other guys we met was Mike Gadd. He's an international winemaker and owner of Wino's, a wine bar and restaurant in the main street. Wino's house wine, his award-winning current vintage red, is served on-tap from a keg! It's a damned good drop, too. Anyway, as Mike seems to know everyone and everything that goes on he said he'd show us around.

We decided to first check out Aaron's kitchen. He soon sorted us out with some duck breasts, great local asparagus and some excellent Shiraz and

Chardonnay. On the way out, Curtis and I spotted this huge fig tree. It was chockers with ripe fruit and Curtis, never one to miss out on an opportunity, suggested I back the truck up. By standing on the back seat, he was able to pick (or nick) a basketful of figs. (Stolen fruit is always the sweetest, I reckon!) The duck breasts and the figs gave Curtis an idea for a recipe; I was still looking.

Next morning we picked up Mike, who was a little quieter than usual. The night before had been the wake for Di Cullen, winemaker extraordinaire and matriarch of the Margaret River region. The Cullen family were the first to plant vines in the region. I'm not certain if Mike's quieter demeanour was the result of his solemnity or the magnums of red that were brought up from the Cullens' cellar for the wake. A little of both, I suspect. Put that many winemakers and that much red together in one place and it's critical mass, party style.

He suggested one stop should be at Cloverdene, Trevor and Debbie Dennis's place in Karridale. As we drove into the property, about thirty plump guineafowl scattered and a gang of kelpies, that quintessential Australian sheepdog, jumped enthusiastically alongside the car. Trev came in from checking a flock of sheep. He explained they had just started milking again — the sheep that is. A shearer by trade, Trevor loves sheep and he and Debbie have combined that love with an interest in biodynamic and organic farming and ended up with a business making sheep's cheese. The traditionally inspired cheeses are full-flavoured — particularly impressive was an aged pecorino. Something to go with asparagus perhaps?

There was just time for a quick surf before we headed back to Vasse Felix to take over Aaron's kitchen. Prep for dinner came and went in a blur. When we were done, we were lucky enough to sit with our new mates out on the verandah overlooking the vineyards as a gentle sea breeze blew away the heat of the day. Curtis's brother and his girlfriend were also able to join us. David Birch, whom we'd met surfing, was still harvesting late into the night but sent along some wine anyway. Now that's the kind of friend I like!

We not only had some new friends to share the beautiful food and wonderful wine with, we had some old ones, too.

Poached asparagus

First, poach the eggs as these can be done in advance, kept in cold water and reheated for serving.

SERVES 4

4 very fresh free-range eggs
1 teaspoon white-wine vinegar
2 teaspoons salt
400 g/14 oz asparagus
100 g/3 1/2 oz Parmigiano Reggiano
*   or pecorino cheese, finely grated*
juice of 1 lemon
200 mL/7 fl oz extra virgin olive oil
freshly ground black pepper
1 head of celery, pale inner leaves only,
*   coarsely chopped*
1/2 cup mint leaves, coarsely chopped

1 Crack each egg into a cup. Fill a deep saucepan with water and bring to the boil. Reduce to a simmer and add the vinegar and 1 teaspoon of salt. Stir with a spoon to make a whirlpool and drop an egg into the centre. Cook until the white is firm and the yolk runny, 3–4 minutes. Remove with a slotted spoon and transfer to a bowl of cold water. Repeat with the remaining eggs.

2 Bring a large saucepan of water to the boil and add 1 teaspoon of salt. Snap off the base of the asparagus spears where they become naturally tender, or trim and peel the ends. Tie into batches of spears of equal thickness and poach until tender, 2–4 minutes, according to their size. It is better if they are tender rather than crunchy. Discard the string.

3 To make the dressing, place the cheese in a bowl and add half the lemon juice. Mash with a spoon to form a paste. Gradually incorporate more lemon juice to give a smooth paste, without it becoming too sharp. Now gradually add the oil in small amounts to give a creamy mayonnaise-like mixture. Season to taste with the black pepper. Alternatively, place dressing ingredients in a food processor and whiz to form a smooth paste. The consistency should be runny but not entirely liquid.

continued over…

4 To serve, gently lower the eggs into the asparagus cooking water to reheat. Toss the asparagus with half of the dressing, coating well. Place on a serving plate. Using a slotted spoon, remove the eggs from the water and place on top of the asparagus. Drizzle the remaining dressing over the eggs and around the plate, then sprinkle the celery leaves and mint on top. Finally, season with more black pepper.

Ben O'Donoghue

Creamy Parmesan and parsley polenta

Polenta is the Italian answer to mashed potato. It is a very versatile dish and can be used wet, like mashed potato, or it can be cooked a little longer and left to set. The polenta can then be cut and grilled, and simply served with a good Napoli sauce as a starter.

SERVES 4

1.2 L/2 pints milk
small sprig of thyme
3 garlic cloves, peeled and crushed with the
    back of a knife
1 fresh bay leaf
125 g/4^1/$_2$ oz polenta (not instant)
25 g/^{3}/$_4$ oz butter
55 g/2 oz freshly grated Parmesan cheese
2 teaspoons chopped flat leaf parsley
nutmeg, to taste
salt and freshly ground black pepper

1. Put the milk, thyme, garlic and bay leaf in a saucepan and bring to the near boil. Strain into a clean pan. Slowly whisk in the polenta. Place back on the heat and continue to whisk until it comes to the boil. Reduce the heat to very low and simmer, stirring often, for 1 hour. The polenta should resemble the consistency of mashed potato. Once it is cooked it will not have a floury taste.

2. Stir in the butter, Parmesan and parsley, and season with nutmeg, salt and pepper to taste.

Curtis Stone

Marinated salmon with oyster fritters and a lemon and yoghurt dressing

Gravlax is originally a Scandinavian dish, which involves marinating salmon in a salty pickle between two stones to intensify the flavour. I don't use two stones but it's important to have a long thin knife to slice the salmon finely.

SERVES 4

1/2 leek, white part only
1 large shallot (eschalot)
1/2 cup loosely packed dill
finely grated zest of 1 orange
finely grated zest of 1 lemon
100 g/3 1/2 oz sugar
100 g/3 1/2 oz sea salt flakes
1 side of fresh salmon, weighing
    about 1 kg/2 lb 4 oz
2 1/2 tablespoons Dijon mustard
150 g/5 1/2 oz finely chopped dill

Dressing
100 g/3 1/2 oz natural yoghurt
3 1/2 tablespoons milk
1 tablespoon lemon juice

Batter
200 mL/7 fl oz beer at room temperature
10 g/1/3 oz fresh yeast
pinch caster sugar
100 g/3 1/2 oz plain flour
salt and freshly ground black pepper

500 mL/18 fl oz vegetable oil, for frying
8 oysters
2–3 tablespoons plain flour

1 Place the leek, shallot, dill, zests, sugar and salt in a food processor and chop well. Rub over both sides of the salmon and wrap tightly with plastic wrap. Place on a tray, and put another tray on top. Weight this and transfer the lot to the refrigerator. Marinate for 24–48 hours.

2 Unwrap the salmon and thoroughly wash off the marinade with water. Pat dry with paper towels and smear the side without skin with Dijon mustard. Press the chopped dill onto the mustard. Slice the salmon into thin strips and arrange, overlapping, on four plates.

3 To make the dressing, whisk the yoghurt and milk together, then whisking constantly, gradually add the lemon juice. Season to taste with salt and pepper.

4 To make the batter, place the beer, yeast and sugar in a bowl and leave in a warm place for 10 minutes. Whisk in the flour gradually, and season with salt and pepper.

5 Heat the oil in a small saucepan. Dust the oysters with the flour, then dip into the batter. Fry, a few at a time, in the hot oil until golden, about 1–2 minutes. Drain on paper towels. Place two oysters on each plate and drizzle the dressing over the salmon for serving.

Curtis Stone

Crab and chilli tagliatelle

Crabmeat is a perfect example of seafood that needs to be kept simple. The flavour works well with a hint of chilli and a little bit of citrus. As the crab has been cooked before it is picked from the shell, it only needs to be reheated in the sauce, making this a very quick dish to prepare.

SERVES 4

5 plum tomatoes
1 tablespoon olive oil
2 shallots (eschalots), finely diced
3 garlic cloves, crushed
1 bird's-eye chilli, finely chopped
200 g/7 oz crabmeat
5 tablespoons dry white wine
500 g/1 lb 2 oz fresh or 400 g/14 oz dried
    tagliatelle
55 g/2 oz butter
2 tablespoons chopped flat leaf parsley
2 tablespoons extra virgin olive oil
1 tablespoon lemon juice
4 sprigs of chervil, to garnish

1. Core the tomatoes, cut a cross on the opposite end then plunge into boiling water and blanch for 12–15 seconds. Remove with a slotted spoon and cool in iced water. Peel and squeeze out any excess moisture, then dice. Reserve.

2. Heat the olive oil in a frying pan. Add the shallot, garlic and chilli, and cook over a moderately low heat until soft, but not browned, 1–2 minutes. Add the crabmeat and cook for 30 seconds. Add the white wine, increase the heat and deglaze. The sauce will reduce while the pasta is cooking.

3. Cook the tagliatelle in boiling salted water for 1–2 minutes, or according to the manufacturer's instructions. Melt the butter with $2^1/_2$ tablespoons of water in a large saucepan. Drain the pasta and place in the pan of butter and water. Toss to coat. Add half the parsley to the pasta, tossing the remainder in with the crab sauce. Stir in the reserved tomatoes, the extra virgin olive oil and the lemon juice.

4. Take a quarter of the pasta and twist it around a roasting fork. Place it in a warmed pasta bowl and gently slide the fork out, leaving a spiral. Repeat with the remaining pasta. Spoon the sauce around the outside and garnish each serve with a sprig of chervil.

Curtis Stone

Peppered duck breast, poached balsamic figs and garlic crisps with jus gras

Duck is a lovely rich meat. The classic 'Duck a la Orange' works so well because the acidity of the citrus fruit cuts through the richness of the duck. In this dish I use instead the acidity of the balsamic. It's important to blanch the slices of garlic so that the flavour is not overpowering.

SERVES 4

3 tablespoons coarsely ground
    black pepper
4 duck breasts, weighing
    about 200 g/7 oz each
250 mL/9 fl oz vegetable oil, for frying
4 ripe figs
250 mL/9 fl oz balsamic vinegar
12 garlic cloves, very thinly sliced
1 L/1³/₄ pints milk
salt
2 cups picked over watercress

1. Preheat the oven to 200°C/400°F/Gas Mark 7. Place the pepper on a plate and firmly press the duck breasts skin-side down into it.

2. Heat 1 tablespoon of the oil in a frying pan with a heatproof handle. Fry the duck breasts, skin-side down, over a medium heat until golden brown, about 4–5 minutes. They should be cooked on the skin-side only to prevent them drying out. Transfer the pan to the oven and bake for 5 minutes. Remove the duck from the oven and allow to rest for 3–5 minutes.

3. Prick the figs with a skewer, then place the figs and balsamic vinegar in a small saucepan. Heat gently for 4–5 minutes, then remove from the heat.

4. Place the garlic in a small saucepan and add one-third of the milk. Bring to the near boil. Strain and return the garlic to the saucepan. Repeat this procedure twice. Pat the garlic dry with paper towel. Heat the remaining oil in a small frying pan and fry the garlic until golden brown, 4–5 minutes. Drain on paper towels and season with salt.

continued over...

Curtis Stone

Peppered duck breast, poached balsamic figs and garlic crisps with jus gras, continued...

5 To serve, slice each breast into five medallions and arrange in a semi-circle on four plates. Slice the figs in half and sit behind the duck. Place a small bunch of watercress and some garlic crisps on either side of the fig, and drizzle a little jus gras over each breast.

Jus gras

YIELDS ABOUT 150 ML/5½ FL OZ

1 kg/2 lb 4 oz chicken wings
4 tablespoons vegetable oil
1 L/1¾ pints chicken stock
75 g/2½ oz shallots (eschalots), sliced
3 garlic cloves, crushed with the back of
*   a knife*
5 white peppercorns
1 sprig of thyme
3 fresh bay leaves

1 Chop each chicken wing into three. Heat the oil in a heavy-based pan and brown the wings over a high heat, 4–5 minutes. Remove the wings from the pan, drain the oil and return the wings to the pan.

2 Add the stock, shallots, garlic, peppercorns, thyme and bay leaves, and slowly bring to the boil. Simmer over a very low heat, uncovered, for 2 hours, or until the stock is rich and reduced to about two-thirds of a cup.

3 Strain into a bowl. Place a heavy pan on top of the wings to squeeze out all the juice, and leave for 30 minutes. Discard the bones. Pass the stock through muslin. If necessary, get rid of the excess fat by chilling the stock; the fat will solidify on top and can be easily taken off.

Curtis Stone

Venison wrapped in copa di forma with porcini mushrooms

Get your butcher and local deli person to do the hard yards by trimming the venison and slicing the copa di forma. It's good to know the size of the venison loin before buying the copa di forma, so go to the butcher first. The deli can then overlap the slices of copa di forma on silicon paper, to a size large enough to cover (roughly three times as wide, and as long as) the meat.

SERVES 4

15 g/$\frac{1}{2}$ oz dried porcini
100 g/3$\frac{1}{2}$ oz unsalted butter
6 field mushrooms, about 250 g/9 oz, sliced
2 garlic cloves, finely chopped
salt and freshly ground black pepper
45 g/1$\frac{1}{2}$ oz fresh breadcrumbs
$\frac{1}{2}$ bunch of thyme
$\frac{1}{2}$ bunch of rosemary
$\frac{1}{2}$ bunch of sage
1 kg/2 lb 4 oz trimmed venison loin
about 250 g/9 oz copa di forma (see above)
250 mL/9 fl oz red wine, such as Shiraz

1 Soak the porcini in boiling water for 10 minutes. Drain, rinse under cold water and squeeze dry. Melt 30 g/1 oz of butter in a frying pan and add the mushrooms. Cook until coloured, then add the porcini and garlic. Cook, stirring, until moist but not dry, 2–3 minutes. Season with salt and pepper, and stir in the breadcrumbs. Set aside to cool.

2 Pick the leaves off the thyme, rosemary and sage. Reserve half. Chop the remainder and sprinkle over the venison with a little pepper.

3 Lie the silicon paper carrying the overlapping slices of copa di forma on a flat surface. Place the venison on top, end to end with the copa di forma. Spread the mushroom mixture along the length of the meat. Starting from one side and using the silicon paper for leverage, roll the copa di forma around the meat to form a sausage. Tie with string in several places to secure.

continued opposite...

④ In a non-stick pan large enough to fit the meat (if this size is unavailable, cut the roll into 4 even portions), melt 45 g/1½ oz of butter. When it starts to foam, add the venison and fry over a gentle heat until crisp and brown on all sides, 12–15 minutes*. Add the reserved herbs and fry until crisp. Transfer the meat and herbs to a plate, cover with foil and leave to rest.

⑤ Pour the wine into the pan, increase the heat and reduce it by half. Turn off the heat and add the last of the butter. Swirl until melted to give a sauce with an intense wine flavour. Slice the venison and serve with the sauce and pot-roasted baby turnips.

*Venison should be served rare to medium but if you like it well done just cook it for 10 minutes longer.

Pot-roasted turnips

I love pot-roasted baby turnips with venison, but you could serve your own favourite vegetable with it. They are equally as good with lamb.

SERVES 4

24 baby turnips
16 garlic cloves, peeled
salt and freshly ground black pepper
30 g/1 oz butter
1 teaspoon white wine vinegar
2 tablespoons chopped flat leaf parsley

① Bring a saucepan of water to the boil and add the turnips, garlic and ½ teaspoon of salt. Simmer gently until the turnips are tender, about 15 minutes. Drain. Add the butter to the pan and heat gently until foaming. Return the turnips and garlic in a single layer and cook over a gentle heat until golden brown, 5–10 minutes. Add the vinegar and parsley, and season to taste with salt and pepper. Serve immediately.

Sparkling strawberry wine jellies

SERVES 6

100 g/3 1/2 oz caster sugar
750 mL/1 bottle strawberry sparkling
*   wine or sparkling rosé, chilled*
2 teaspoons/6 leaves gelatine
500 g/1 lb 2 oz ripe strawberries
1 tablespoon chopped borage or mint
2 tablespoons peeled, seeded and
*   chopped cucumber, white flesh only*
1 tablespoon icing sugar
crème fraîche or sour cream, to serve

1. Place the sugar and 5 tablespoons of the wine in a medium saucepan. Stir gently over a low heat to dissolve the sugar. Soak the gelatine in cold water until soft, then squeeze dry. Add to the saucepan and stir until dissolved.

2. Reserve half a punnet of strawberries for a coulis and six strawberries to decorate. Core and roughly chop the remainder. Place in a bowl with the borage and cucumber and lightly toss to combine. Distribute between six cappuccino cups or six 200 mL/7 fl oz moulds.

3. Stir the remaining strawberry wine into the gelatine mixture and gently pour over the fruit. Place on a small tray for easy handling and put into the freezer to chill rapidly. When they begin to set, transfer to the refrigerator to fully set.

4. To make the coulis, purée the reserved half punnet of strawberries with the icing sugar and pass through a sieve.

5. To serve, place the moulds into hot water for a couple of seconds to loosen, then turn out onto a plate. Serve with the coulis, crème fraîche and the reserved strawberries.

Ben O'Donoghue

Mascarpone and raspberry crème brûlée

This is a sweet creamy classic from France. I love mascarpone cheese and think the tartness of the raspberries breaks up the consistency a little. If you don't have a gas burner you can caramelise the sugar under a hot grill.

SERVES 4

2 tablespoons milk
450 mL/³/₄ pint double cream
1 vanilla pod, split in half lengthways
3 free-range egg yolks
1 whole free-range egg
75 g/2¹/₂ oz caster sugar
250 g/9 oz mascarpone cheese
12 raspberries
2 tablespoons demerera sugar

❶ Place the milk, cream and vanilla pod in a medium saucepan and slowly bring to the near boil.

❷ In a clean saucepan, lightly hand-whisk the egg-yolks, egg and sugar together until creamy. Gradually add the mascarpone, whisking constantly.

❸ Pour the milk over the egg mixture and stir to combine. Place over a low heat and whisk constantly until the mixture thickens and coats the back of a wooden spoon. Strain into a jug.

❹ Place 3 raspberries in the bottom of 4 thick martini glasses. Pour the crème mixture over the top. Transfer to the refrigerator to set overnight.

❺ Sprinkle the surfaces evenly with the sugar. Preheat the griller to hot and place the crèmes under the heat until the sugar melts and caramelises.

❻ Serve when cooled a little.

Curtis Stone

Bellarine Peninsula

Bellarine Peninsula

Mussels, Zen and Spice Girl

Curtis Stone

The Bellarine Peninsula, just a sixty-minute drive from Melbourne, extends from Geelong to Queenscliffe and down to Torquay, just before Bells Beach on the Surf Coast. The peninsula offers both protected bay outlooks and beaches, as well as spectacular ocean vistas and excellent surf. This is where I did some of my growing up.

So what can I tell you about my peninsula? Well, the Geelong region grew prosperous through servicing the needs of the wool-growers and squatters who thrived around the peninsula area and into the hinterland in the mid-nineteenth century. Queenscliffe, at the western edge of the entrance to the massive Port Phillip Bay, initially became best known as the home of the pilot service which from 1838 guided ships through the reefs and the narrow entrance into the bay. Because of the dangerous tides at the entrance it became known as 'the rip'. In the 1850s a lighthouse and lifeboat rescue service were added. This coincided with a massive increase in the number of ships arriving due to the discovery of gold not far inland at Ballarat and Bendigo. Ships, filled to overflowing with hopefuls from all over the world, landed almost every day. In the 1800s, for some reason fearing an attack from the Russians, massive cannons were installed at the western and eastern entrance to the bay. The attack never came and the cannons were rarely, if ever, fired in anger. In the late 1800s, holiday-makers sailed across the bay in ferries and boats from Melbourne to holiday at Queenscliffe. Many beautiful, grand Victorian hotels and guesthouses sprang up and are still patronised to this day.

While little appears to have changed in Queenscliffe, west along the coast through Barwon Heads and down to Torquay much has changed as holiday-makers, and especially surfers, take advantage of the spectacular coastline and consistent surf. The peninsula today has also become a magnet for foodies, gourmet producers and quality wines. The mild climate makes the region ideal for growing all manner of produce. There's local mussels, shellfish such as scallops and lobster, plus fish from Port Phillip Bay and the wild seas of Bass Strait. In addition,

Bacchus Marsh

Melton

MELBOURNE

Meredith

PORT PHILLIP BAY

Portarlington

Corio Bay

Lozza and Golly's ■

■ *Scotchman's Hill*

GEELONG

*Bellarine
Peninsula*

• *Moriac*

Barwon
Heads

Queenscliff

*Thirteenth
Beach*

Bellbrae •

Torquay
■ *Bells Beach*

there is beef and lamb, rabbit, duck, poultry, game and cheeses, even buffalo mozzarella. Plus there are some fantastic vineyards that produce some of my favourite wines. Let's take a short tour of some of what we discovered.

First, family. We called in to see my mother Lorraine (Lozza) and Golly. (His real name's Shane but my brother, Luke, and I have always called him Golly because he used to have thick curly black hair.) In Lozza and Golly's back-yard there is a large and lush herb garden, as well as the last of some fresh rhubarb and seasonal vegetables. I introduced Bender to Donald and Daisy, the pet ducks. The ducks sat unperturbed on their pond (well, actually, bath-tub set in the ground) while I stirred Lozza about how good they'd taste roasted and served in a red wine jus …

What I observed about this homecoming was that it is not only the young or the herbal types living in Nimbin, Margaret River and so on, who are into recycling, rediscovering and redefining their lives. There was evidence of a quiet revolution everywhere — Lozza and Golly are living a more natural and simpler existence with their chooks and ducks providing free-range eggs, and an organic herb and veggie patch I'd kill for. Golly puts his boat into the bay at the foot of our street to catch fresh fish. In some aspects, they're almost self-sufficient.

After dropping in on Lozza and Golly, Bender and I headed out for the surf. While Bender thinks that Margaret River is the epitome of the surfing scene, I wanted to show him my neck of the woods. Bells Beach is a little out of my league (the best surfers in the world don't come here to compete in the Ripcurl Masters for nothing), but Thirteenth Beach about fifteen minutes from Lozza's is always consistent and offers a wave on most days. On the day we went it wasn't as big as it can get, but it did offer a fun time in the waves so we grabbed the boards and headed on in.

As usual a good wave acts like a magnet and we headed over to where a group had already gathered. On the peninsula it's not unusual to drive along the parking areas and see pick-up after pick-up parked side-by-side. The locals know that on a big surf day, you won't be able to get a tradesman for love or money. That's the situation for many similar seaside towns. In management jargon, I think that's called prioritising. I'd love to have that attitude, but I enjoy what I do so much that I guess all that other stuff will have to stay on the backburner for a while.

Out in the surf there was a whole bunch of different people. After we'd said g'day, we ended up talking to a bunch of foodies who all seemed to have taken a leaf out of the tradesmen's books. We caught a few waves over the next hour or so and told them we're back home for Lozza's wedding anniversary. Grant Hutchins of The Heads restaurant immediately offered the use of his kitchen and part of the restaurant for the party. As they have a dishwasher and Mum doesn't, we thought this was a good idea. The restaurant was perfect — casual and stylish — and, perched over the river, it had a view to die for.

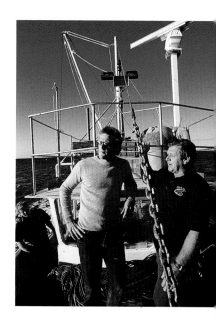

Apparently The Heads is quite famous because it was Diver Dan's home in the television programme 'Sea Change'. This didn't have any impact on Bender and me as we've been away for around six years each and had completely missed the programme. We later found out that Lozza loved the show and loved the idea of having the celebration there. We now had to source some local produce. Where better to start than with the people we met surfing?

In the small town of Bellbrae (just north of Bells Beach), Albie Cachia and her husband Gerrard run The Screaming Seeds Spice Company. Walk inside and the air is thick with the aromas of exciting blends. Albie constantly applies her Mediterranean instincts to guide her while trying out new spice combinations. She is also using Australian native outback blends, which include lemon myrtle and Dorrigo pepper. Albie and Gerrard are not afraid to experiment and invent new taste sensations.

Zen's makes largely Italian-style breads. Danny Zen's ciabatta are infused with olives, basil or roasted vegetables. The bakery is a family affair. Father Giannni came to the region from Padua in the Veneto and started the Belmont bakery almost 50 years ago, bringing the Italian traditions with him. Danny now bakes the bread while sister Gabrielle runs the front of house.

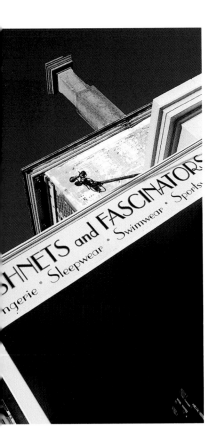

Danny suggested we call into a local provender, Warren and Hutch, so named because the owners, Sarah and Jane, had originally owned a rabbit farm of the same name. Jane had previously attended a Cordon Bleu school in England and Sarah had been involved in promoting Australian produce throughout the UK — so food and wine are definitely in their blood.

They met us at the door wearing starched aprons and warm smiles. Inside the store, Bender and I got into a conversation about what was fresh. Bender chose some plump free-range hens for the party, which he intended to prepare with Albie's spices. Sarah and Jane know everything about everything food-wise and who does what in the region.

They mentioned that Bob Grant was worth a visit. He's an apiarist, but not a typical one. While many of his hives are out in the countryside, he has three hives set out in the backyard of his welding shop. Bob explained that the suburbs are one of the best places for hives because bees need flowers and suburban gardens are chock-full of flowering plants, shrubs and trees. Another surprising fact: pure honey is a powerful antibiotic. In countries such as Russia, honey has been used as a medication for centuries. This reminded me of a conversation we'd had with Baamba in Broome about how traditional Aboriginals collected bush honey to treat cuts or scratches. Bob also told us another fact: if the seal on a honeycomb is unbroken it can keep for over a century! Isn't nature full of surprises?

Apparently the honey industry in Australia is unique compared to the northern hemisphere where almost all the honey production is from ground and meadow flowers. Here, due to the prolifically flowering gums and native plants, such as grevillia, almost all our honey is from flowering trees that are high in pollen content and goodness.

Earlier, Lozza had suggested if we wanted fresh mussels we should get along and see Wayne Senior (known as Mr Mussels) and Wayne Junior on the Portarlington Pier. On the peninsula most things are no further than ten or fifteen minutes apart, and a short drive later we are at the pier in Portarlington. Wayne and Wayne were just preparing to go and harvest some of their mussels so we hitched a ride. We figured we wouldn't be able to get mussels any fresher if we pulled them ourselves.

As baby hatchlings, mussels are funnelled into a stocking-like casing (similar to making sausages) where a long rope runs through the centre from top to bottom. The casing holds the mussels against the rope long enough for the mussels to attach themselves by their own foot. There they remain for the rest of their lives, growing plump and tender. The ropes of mussels are hung from long lines between buoys just a five-minute boat ride out into Corio Bay. Bender and I pulled some in ourselves. It's a completely natural way of farming — wild product with no messing about or adding anything unnatural. The mussels live in the clean tidal water and filter-feed naturally. When they are ready, they are harvested and can be on the table in just a few hours.

On the way back to the restaurant we called into Scotchman's Hill winery, which has been making wines since the mid 1800s. The winery sits proud on a hill overlooking Corio Bay where Melbourne city can be seen on the other side of the bay. We took some of their Cabernet Sauvignon and Chardonnay for the guests.

Ben and I headed back to Grant's restaurant and started to cook. And it wasn't long before I found out something I hadn't suspected about my mother before now — she's a dirty rotten sneak. I reckon of all the people in the world, you really should be able to trust your mates and your mum.

The reason (I thought) Bender and I were in the Bellarine Peninsula was to cook a special meal to celebrate Lozza and Golly's wedding anniversary. Mum had suggested it, I had gone along with it, and Bender had agreed to help out. Lozza had told me that she was inviting a lot of her new friends who've moved into the neighbourhood and that I wouldn't know anyone, but it would be good for me to meet them. Occasionally I'd pop out of the kitchen to check on the arrival of these guests, but even as the appointed hour drew near no one had arrived. I should have smelt a rat, but being the honest, believable and, as it turned out, gullible soul that I am, I was completely in the dark.

Eventually Mum announced that all her friends were there and, not wishing to overcook the meal, Bender and I plated-up and headed into the restaurant to serve. But, rather than a whole table of Mum's cronies there sat just about all of my best friends, none of whom I'd been able to catch up with since I'd been in Australia. They had flown in from Queensland and Tasmania; and some had driven from the country, one had even cut short footy training. (Considering he was voted Best on Ground two days later, perhaps he should try that more often!)

It was a brilliant surprise and, as it turned out, everyone, even Bender and Grant, the restaurant owner, had been in on it. I did feel like an idiot, but a happy one. Great food. Great friends. Even when you've been away for almost six years, your mates are your mates for life. What else is there?

Well, there's always footy, and after another kick in the backyard with Bender, I snuck off to watch my brother play for his Aussie Rules amateur team, East Keilor. It's great to catch up with family and friends, and experience the simple pleasures — like having a beer at the footy with your brother. Something I don't get to do as often as I'd like.

Buffalo mozzarella, broad bean, mint and rocket salad

I cannot think of anything I would rather eat during summer than this beautiful salad. It captures the freshness that represents everything about that season to me. As an option you can shave some cheese over the salad at the end to garnish, but I find the pale green, white and jagged dark green of the rocket appealing enough.

SERVES 4–6

300 g/11 oz shelled small broad beans*
salt
75 g/2 ¾ oz pecorino cheese, freshly grated
2 tablespoons chopped mint
juice of 1 lemon
freshly ground black pepper
5 tablespoons extra virgin olive oil
3 fresh buffalo mozzarella balls, weighing
*   about 250 g/9 oz***
2 cups loosely packed wild rocket
2 tablespoons mint leaves, torn if large

❶ Place the broad beans in a mortar and pestle with a little salt and smash to a rough, chunky paste. Add the pecorino cheese, half the chopped mint and three-quarters of the lemon juice. Season to taste and toss to combine. Add enough olive oil, about 3 tablespoons, to make the mixture loose and wet.

❷ Break the mozzarella into pieces and place on a serving plate. Top with half of the broad bean mixture. Combine the rocket and mint leaves with the remaining lemon juice and olive oil. Scatter over the mozzarella. Dress with the remaining broad bean mixture and black pepper.

* As the broad beans are uncooked in this salad, only those that are fresh, young and small should be used. If unavailable, substitute with 450 g/1 lb mature or frozen ones. These will need to be blanched for 1 minute and shelled.
** The equivalent weight of bocconcini (cows' milk mozzarella) can be substituted.

Marinated mussel salad

Curtis reckons the mussels in Port Phillip Bay are the best in Australia and, you know, he was close. It doesn't matter where the best mussels come from, just get the freshest ones you can find. If they're closed and heavy then they're alive, and if they smell good and don't float in water, you're pretty well onto some fresh mussels. Mussels that are dead or that have been out of water for too long can be bloody lethal. This salad is ideal for a hot summer's lunch, starter or part of a barbecue spread.

SERVES 4–6

2 kg/4 1/2 lb live fresh black mussels
500 g/1 lb 2 oz mixed fresh tomatoes
    (red and yellow cherry, vine,
    green stripey)
salt and freshly ground black pepper
1 garlic clove, finely sliced
1 bunch of coriander
100 mL/3 1/2 fl oz ponzu sauce*
1/2 teaspoon grated ginger
1 tablespoon soft palm sugar
2–3 green chillies, deseeded and sliced
    into thin strips
200 g/7 oz honeydew melon,
    peeled and diced

1 Clean the mussels by pulling off the hairy beard, then rinsing in cold water. Discard any that float. Heat a heavy-based saucepan until hot, then add just enough mussels to cover the bottom. Splash a little water over the top and quickly cover with the lid. When they have opened, remove and drain in a colander. Discard any that have not opened. Repeat this process until all the mussels are cooked. Allow to cool.

2 Extract the mussels from the shell and reserve, discarding the shells. Cut the tomatoes as you please; the smaller ones in half, larger ones into chunks or irregular shapes. Place in a large bowl and season with salt and pepper. Add the garlic.

3 Finely slice the coriander roots and mix with the ponzu sauce, ginger and palm sugar. Add to the tomatoes, along with the reserved mussels. Taste for salt and pepper. Rest in the refrigerator until required, at least two hours.

4 Add the coriander leaves, chilli and melon to the mussel mixture. Serve either as one big salad, or individually plated.

* To make the ponzu sauce, combine 2 teaspoons rice vinegar, 3 tablespoons lime juice, 2 teaspoons mirin, 2 tablespoons dashi and 3 tablespoons soy sauce. Leave in the refrigerator overnight before use.

Spiced mussel and saffron soup

This is a soup that I picked up from the master, Marco Pierre White. I have altered it slightly but it is very much his creation. Don't worry about throwing away the mussels after you strain the soup. You have cooked all the flavour and juice out of them, so you are not wasting food — better yet, if you have a cat you will be a popular person.

SERVES 6

2 large pinches of saffron threads
750 mL/1 bottle dry white wine
55 g/2 oz butter
1 onion, thinly sliced
1 stalk of celery, thinly sliced
1 leek, sliced
1 teaspoon curry powder
1 teaspoon cayenne pepper
2 fresh bay leaves
1 sprig of thyme
2.5 kg/5¹/₂ lb mussels, scrubbed and debearded
500 mL/18 fl oz fish stock
450 mL/³/₄ pint pouring cream
salt and freshly ground black pepper

1. Melt the butter in a large pot, then add the onion, celery, leek, curry powder, cayenne pepper, bay leaves, thyme and saffron. Cook for 5–6 minutes, over a low heat, bleeding colour from the saffron.

2. Once the vegetables are soft, add the mussels, give them a good stir and cover the pot. Cook until opened, about 1 min-ute. Discard those that haven't opened, and reserve 6–18 (depending on their size) to garnish. Add the remaining white wine, bring to the boil over a high heat and cook for 8–10 minutes. Add the fish stock, and bring to the boil. Reduce heat to low and simmer for 10 minutes. Add the cream and return to the near boil.

3. Strain the soup through a colander, then through a sieve lined with muslin. Season to taste with salt and pepper. Extract the meat from most of the mussels and discard the shells. Retain some in their shells to garnish the soup. To serve, ladle the soup into bowls and add the mussels.

Curtis Stone

Spaghettini vongole

This recipe originates from the south of Italy where the clams are wonderful. In Australia we are privileged to have access to some of the best seafood in the world so we should take advantage of it. Serve with some crusty bread so you can sop up the sauce.

SERVES 4

300 g/11 oz dried spaghettini
sea salt
1¹/₂ tablespoons olive oil
1 shallot (eschalot), finely diced
2 bird's-eye chillies, deseeded and finely chopped
2 garlic cloves, crushed
600 g/1 lb 5 oz fresh clams (vongole)
2¹/₂ tablespoons dry white wine
8 cherry tomatoes
1 tablespoon tapenade*
3 teaspoons baby capers
45 g/1¹/₂ oz anchovies, finely chopped
¹/₂ cup chopped flat leaf parsley
5 tablespoons extra virgin olive oil
juice of 1 lemon
freshly ground black pepper
75 g/2³/₄ oz butter
2¹/₂ tablespoons water
4 sprigs of chervil, to garnish

① Preheat the oven to 220°C/425°F/Gas Mark 8. Bring a large pot of water to the boil. Add the spaghettini, a big pinch of salt and 1 tablespoon of the olive oil. Cook until al dente, about 6 minutes.

② Meanwhile, heat 2 teaspoons of the olive oil in a large saucepan and add the shallot and the chilli. Fry without browning for 30 seconds. Add the garlic, stir for 10 seconds, then add the clams and the wine. Immediately cover and shake the pan. Cook for 1¹/₂ minutes.

③ Place the tomatoes on a baking tray and drizzle with the remaining olive oil. Place in the oven for 5–6 minutes or until they start to burst.

④ Once the clams start to open, add the tapenade, capers, anchovies and half the parsley. Shake the pan to ensure that everything is well mixed. Remove from the heat and stir in the extra virgin olive oil and lemon juice. Season to taste with pepper.

continued opposite...

* Tapenade can be purchased at delicatessens and large supermarkets.

Curtis Stone

5. Melt the butter and the water in a large pan. Drain the pasta and mix in the butter and water emulsion. Add the remaining parsley. Curl a quarter of the pasta around a roasting fork. When it is tightly in place, gently ease the spiral of pasta into the centre of a serving bowl. Repeat with the remaining pasta. Arrange the clams around the pasta and drizzle over the sauce. Place the tomatoes on the side of each bowl, and garnish with a sprig of chervil. Serve at once.

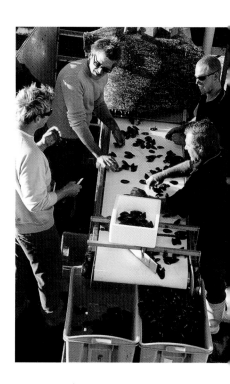

Curtis Stone

Spiced smoky barbecued chicken with a tomato and garlic relish

I developed this recipe for my kettle barbecue. I love the flavours that it imparts to food, and the social theatre that is imparted by this recipe will leave your friends with no doubt as to your creative finesse. The combination of smoke and spice is one that appears across cultures from the Caribbean to Coogee beach. You can use any type of spice combination that rocks your boat. We were lucky enough to come across a great spice shop in Bellbrae and I could not resist their Kashmir-inspired curry mixture.

SERVES 4

*2 garlic cloves, peeled and coarsely
    chopped*
salt
finely grated zest and juice of 2 lemons
*2 tablespoons Kashmiri spice mixture,
    or good quality curry powder*
*1 dried bird's-eye chilli, deseeded and
    crushed*
3¹/₂ tablespoons olive oil
freshly ground black pepper
1.4 kg/3 lb organic chicken
2 bunches of rosemary
1–2 bunches of fresh bay leaves
2 bunches of thyme

1. Smash the garlic with a little salt in a mortar. Add the zest and half of the lemon juice. Add the spice mixture, chilli, oil and black pepper to taste. Mix to a moist paste, adding a little more oil if necessary. This step can also be done in a mini food processor.

2. Remove the excess fat from inside the chicken. Starting from the tail end, carefully separate the skin from the meat by sliding your hand under the skin and gently lifting. Being careful not to break the skin, use scissors to snip the membrane that runs along the centre breast and backbone. Push the spice paste into the cavity you have made between the meat and skin and smear it over the meat.

3. Preheat a kettle or covered barbecue. When the coals have just turned an ashen white colour but are still whole, place the chicken breast-up directly onto the rack and season well with pepper. Close the lid and cook until the chicken starts to colour, 5–7 minutes. Remove the chicken and reduce the heat to low.

continued opposite...

④ Make a bed on the rack using the rosemary, bay leaves and thyme. Place the chicken breast-up on top. Drizzle the remaining lemon juice over the chicken and replace the lid; the herbs will start to smoke. Keep the lid on and cook for 40–45 minutes, or until the chicken juices run clear when the base of the leg is pieced. Don't open the lid too often, or you will lose the smoke. Allow to rest for 10–15 minutes before tucking in.

Spicy barbecued tomato, garlic and shallot relish

MAKES 1½–2 CUPS

5 long red cayenne chillies
10 small Thai pink shallots (Asian shallots),
    or 5 large, unpeeled
10 garlic cloves, unpeeled
10 large cherry tomatoes
about 1 tablespoon red wine vinegar
about 1 tablespoon olive oil
salt and freshly ground black pepper

① Heat the barbecue or grill to hot. Prick the chillies with a fork and char-grill until the skin blackens and blisters. When cool, peel and deseed.

② Place the shallots and garlic cloves onto the grill and cook over a medium heat until soft. Don't worry if they turn black on the outside because you will be using only the soft inside flesh. Char-grill the tomatoes until soft and the skin splits.

③ Squeeze the soft flesh from the shallots, garlic cloves and tomatoes into a mortar. Add the chillies and pound into a coarse relish. Add enough vinegar and oil to give a good relish consistency, then season with salt and pepper. This step can be done in a mini food processor. Store in the refrigerator, covered, for up to 1 week.

Ben O'Donoghue

Roast saddle of rabbit with baby leeks and asparagus

My uncle used to take my brother and me hunting for rabbits when we were kids. Wild rabbits are usually smaller and the meat is a little tougher, so they can be trickier to cook. Tame or domestic rabbits are quite tender and are relatively inexpensive. If you have not tried them, have a go — roast the saddles and braise the legs.

SERVES 4

4 small rabbits, each weighing
    about 1 kg/2 lb 4 oz, cleaned
2 tablespoons olive oil
2 shallots (eschalots), chopped
1 sprig of thyme
3 fresh bay leaves
2 L/3¹/₂ pints chicken stock
1 tablespoon double/thick cream
30 g/1 oz butter, cubed
salt and freshly ground black pepper
20 spears asparagus, trimmed*
20 baby leeks, trimmed*

* Trim the asparagus and leeks to a similar size.

1. Remove the legs from the rabbits and chop them into four pieces using a cleaver or poultry shears. Heat 1 tablespoon of oil in a heavy-based saucepan and brown the legs over a moderately high heat. Pour off the fat. Add the shallot, thyme and bay leaves and cook for 3–5 minutes. Add the stock, increase the heat and stir to deglaze the pan.

2. Reduce heat and simmer, uncovered, until reduced by three-quarters, about 40 minutes. Strain into a smaller saucepan. Add the cream and simmer gently for 2–3 minutes. Add the butter, cube by cube, whisking well after each addition, until the butter melts. Season to taste and keep warm.

3. Preheat the oven to 200°C/400°F/Gas Mark 7. Remove the belly flaps from the rabbits and reserve. Heat the remaining oil in a cast-iron or flameproof baking pan and fry the saddles over a high heat until golden brown on all sides. Push them to one side and spread out the belly flaps in the pan. Place the saddles on top and transfer to the oven. Roast for 5 minutes. Remove from the pan and rest for 5 minutes.

continued over...

Curtis Stone

4 Cut the belly flaps into thin strips and return to the hot pan. Fry over a high heat until crispy. Drain on paper towels.

5 Bring a large saucepan of salted water to the boil. Cook the asparagus until just tender, about 2 minutes. Remove with a slotted spoon and keep warm. Add the leeks and simmer until al dente, 2–3 minutes. Drain and keep warm.

6 Remove the fillets from the saddles and slice on an angle. Arrange each fillet on a serving plate in a fan. Build a lattice of five asparagus spears and five leeks per plate behind the rabbit, and drizzle with sauce. To serve, garnish with the strips of belly flap.

Curtis Stone

Rabbit with chickpeas, rosemary, garlic and preserved lemon

Rabbits, once the scourge of Australia and hapless speed humps on country roads, now enjoy a place of pride in my repertoire. I love cooking rabbit: the meat has a subtle flavour and a wonderful tender texture — and it's cheap. This recipe uses big flavours to lift the subtlety of the rabbit, and it's simple to do. Rabbit is ideal with steamed spinach or creamy mashed potatoes.

SERVES 4

2 x 1.5 kg/3 lb 5 oz rabbits (ask
    your butcher to joint them into legs,
    shoulders and two saddle cuts)
100 g/3^1/$_2$ oz seasoned flour
5 tablespoons olive oil
20 garlic cloves, peeled
^{1}/$_2$ cup picked rosemary leaves
300 mL/10^1/$_2$ fl oz dry white wine
1 L/1^3/$_4$ pints chicken stock
200 g/7 oz drained canned chickpeas
2 pieces preserved lemon rind, sliced*
salt and freshly ground black pepper

❶ Dredge the rabbit joints in the seasoned flour. Shake off the excess. Heat 3 tablespoons of oil in a large heavy-based flameproof pot or Dutch oven and fry the rabbit, in batches, until golden brown. Remove from the pan. Drain off excess oil and wipe out the burnt flour with paper towels.

❷ Preheat the oven to 180°C/350°F/Gas Mark 5. Reheat the pan and add the remaining oil. Replace the rabbit joints. Add the garlic cloves and rosemary, and fry for a minute or two to develop the flavours. Add the wine, stock, chickpeas and preserved lemon. Bring to a simmer and cover with baking paper, then the lid.

❸ Transfer to the oven and bake for 40 minutes. To check that the rabbit is cooked, press the flesh with your fingers; it should give way under pressure. Remove the rabbit from the pot. Reduce the cooking juices over a moderately high flame until they coat the back of a spoon. Season to taste with salt and pepper. Return the rabbit to the sauce, reheat and serve.

Jars of preserved lemon can be found in delicatessens and large supermarkets.

Grilled T-bone steak with garlic and anchovy butter

I have always loved cooking meat on the bone. The meat keeps a certain kind of sweetness, and lends itself to a relaxed style of eating — or perhaps it's just me who loves gnawing on the bone. I also find that anchovies work particularly well with hearty meats, such as beef or lamb.

SERVES 4

250 g/9 oz unsalted butter, softened
2 garlic cloves, crushed
3 lightly salted anchovy fillets,
    finely chopped
1 large shallot (eschalot), finely chopped
2 tablespoons finely chopped flat
    leaf parsley
salt and freshly ground black pepper
1 tablespoon olive oil
4 x 450 g/1 lb T-bone steaks
5 large field mushrooms, thickly sliced
2¹/₂ tablespoons Worcestershire sauce
4 anchovy fillets, halved lengthways,
    to garnish

❶ Place the butter, garlic, anchovies, shallot and parsley in a large bowl, and season with salt and pepper. Beat together until smooth. Take a large sheet of plastic wrap and spoon the butter in a rough log shape towards one end. Roll up the butter, pressing it into a firm, thick sausage as you go. Roll the sausage on the bench to give a smooth surface, then transfer to the refrigerator to harden.

❷ Brush the steaks with the oil. Fry in a hot pan over a moderately high heat for 2–3 minutes on each side, or to your liking. Cut off four discs of butter and place one on top of each steak. Remove the pan and rest the steak for 3–4 minutes in a warm place before serving.

❸ Meanwhile, heat another pan and get it very hot. Add the mushrooms and Worcestershire sauce. Stir to deglaze for 1–2 minutes. Stack the mushrooms in the centre of four serving plates and place a T-bone on top of each pile. Place two strips of anchovy in a cross on the steaks, and serve.

Note: Any unused butter will keep in the refrigerator for up to 10 days, or in the freezer for 3 months.

Curtis Stone

Citrus and honey almond cake

It was great to hear Curtis's mum telling stories of how he used to love sucking on their local honeycomb when he was a kid, so I thought that in tribute to the big sucker I'd make a suitable cake in his honour.

SERVES 8

200 g/7 oz honey
250 g/9 oz unsalted butter, softened
3 free-range eggs
500 g/1 lb 2 oz ground almonds
1 tablespoon baking powder
finely grated zest and juice each of
*   1 medium orange, 1 lemon and 1 lime*
icing sugar, for dusting

1 Preheat the oven to 150°C/300°F/Gas Mark 3. Grease a 25 cm/10 in springform tin and line with baking paper. Warm the honey in hot water or in a microwave oven without it getting too hot. Place in a large bowl and add the butter, beating until it is thoroughly combined. Add the eggs, one at a time, beating well after each addition.

2 Stir in the almond meal and baking powder. Add the zest and juice of the orange, lemon and lime, and mix until evenly combined. Pour the mix into the prepared tin. Bake in the oven for 1½ hours, or until a small knife inserted into the centre comes out clean. Cool completely in the tin, then turn out and dust with icing sugar.

Ben O'Donoghue

Rhubarb tarte fine with honey and cinnamon ice-cream

My mum grows rhubarb in her garden, so I have always had a soft spot for it. I think it has a lovely tart taste that is perfectly matched with something sweet and a little spicy — the honey and cinnamon ice-cream is the perfect complement. Alternatively, buy some good quality vanilla ice-cream and soften it a little. Mix some ground cinnamon and honey into it and serve.

SERVES 4

200 g/7 oz block puff pastry
6 stalks of rhubarb, very finely sliced on the diagonal to about 1 mm thick and 6–7.5 cm/ 2¹/₂–3 in in length

1. Preheat the oven to 200°C/400°F/Gas Mark 7, and line a baking tray with baking paper. On a lightly floured surface, roll out the puff pastry to a thickness of about ¹/₂ cm/¹/₄ in. Cut out a neat circle 20 cm/8 in in diameter and transfer to the prepared tray.

2. Using a sharp knife, make even cuts (5 mm/¹/₄ in long) through the rim of the pastry at regular intervals, right around the perimeter. Fill the tart by arranging the rhubarb slices on top in a circular pattern. Place a piece of baking paper over the tarte, followed by a second baking tray to weigh down the rhubarb. Transfer to the oven and bake for 25–30 minutes, or until the pastry is golden (it doesn't puff because of the weight) and the rhubarb cooked. Cut into quarters and serve each with a scoop of Honey and Cinnamon Ice-cream.

continued over...

Curtis Stone

Honey and cinnamon ice-cream

SERVES 6–8

200 mL/7 fl oz cream
300 mL/10¹/₂ fl oz milk
1¹/₂ tablespoons caster sugar
1 teaspoon ground cinnamon
1 vanilla pod, split in half lengthways
¹/₂ teaspoon grated nutmeg
1 clove
7 free-range egg yolks
125 g/4¹/₂ oz honey

1. Put the cream and a cup of the milk in a large saucepan. Add the sugar, cinnamon, vanilla pod, nutmeg and clove. Place over a moderate heat and bring to just below boiling.

2. In a bowl, beat the remaining milk with the egg yolks and honey until smooth. Add the milk mixture, whisking constantly. Pour everything back into the saucepan and return to the heat. Cook over a low heat, whisking, until slightly thickened. Strain into a shallow bowl and chill.

3. Once cold, transfer the mixture to an ice-cream machine and churn until semi set. Remove and freeze.

Curtis Stone

Byron Bay

Byron Bay

Beaches, Nuts and Babes

Ben O'Donoghue

Byron Bay, with its epic beaches of crystal-clear water and amazing views of Mount Warning and the rolling hills of the hinterland, is one of the centres of Australia's counter-culture. Hippies, ferals, surfers, organic farmers and tourists flock to this naturally beautiful region where the rainforest meets the sea. It's a zoo!

Cape Byron is the most easterly point of Australia and the lighthouse on the headland is a famous landmark. Byron is also famous as a place for whale watching during the season from June to September — ironically, because whaling was one of Australia's first industries, and a whaling station operated at Byron Bay until 1962.

I first went to Byron Bay with a bunch of mates on the way back from a music festival in Brisbane; it was all a bit of a blur. The next time I went was to meet Peter, my girlfriend's father, so I was a little better behaved.

The reason we were there this time was simple. My partner De-arne was returning to Byron Bay to see her dad and to join up with Curtis and me. With her was our twelve-week-old beautiful baby, Ruby. Curtis and I had planned this food discovery trip for a long time and when Dee and I knew we were going to have a baby, it was she who insisted we carry our plans through. No wonder I love her so much.

I had been with Dee in London for Ruby's birth and her first month. When it was time to leave, I couldn't believe how difficult it was. I couldn't let go at the airport and thought of them, over and over, every day. Just before I left London I got one of those right-trendy mobile phones that can receive photos, and almost every day Dee had been emailing me a new pic of Ruby so that I could feel connected. In the short time I'd been away, Ruby had discovered her vocal

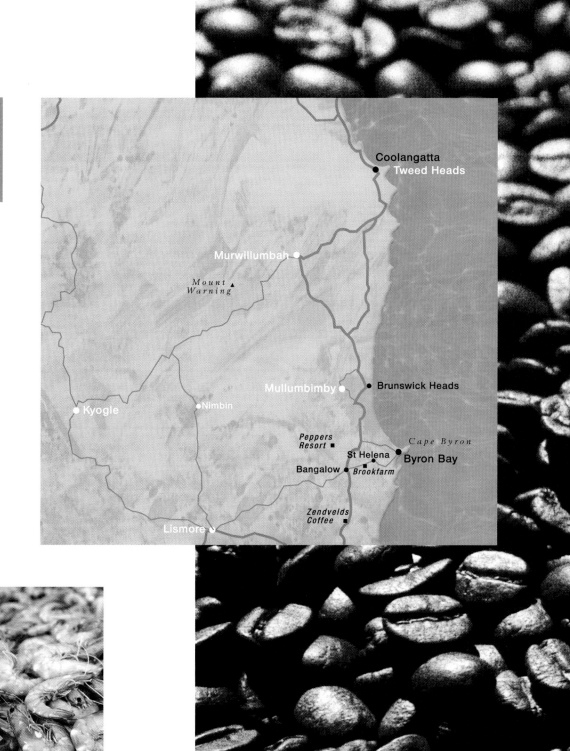

Coolangatta
Tweed Heads

Murwillumbah ●

Mount Warning ▲

Mullumbimby ● ● Brunswick Heads

Kyogle ● ● Nimbin

Peppers Resort ■

St Helena ● *Cape Byron*

Bangalow ● ● Byron Bay
Brookfarm ■

Zendvelds Coffee ■

Lismore ●

cords. Dee would put her on the phone to 'Arrh' and 'Oooh' and tug at my heartstrings. Curtis always knew when I'd been talking to them as I think I must have looked a little misty.

Curtis and I flew into Coolangatta airport. The flight seemed to take forever. At the airport we found Dee and a sleeping Ruby waiting. I couldn't stop looking at Ruby, even though she didn't wake up once. I hoped she was like that every night …

We were planning to cater for a casual family get-together to celebrate Ruby's birth. That meant Curtis and I needed to jump into a car and find some fresh local produce. Oh, and if it was nap time for Ruby, maybe we could squeeze in a surf or two in one of the most beautiful locations in the country.

Bright and early in the morning, Curtis banged on my door, stumbling in from a big night out. He had noticed that one of the trawlers at Brunswick Heads, just up the coast, had come in, and suggested we jump in the car and go down and see what they had. That boy's got stamina!

Brunswick Heads is an idyllic seaside village where fishing boats and trawlers are protected by a natural harbour. We got there just as they'd finished unloading. There were some good-sized eastern tiger prawns and Ted and Bruce, the fishermen, reckoned we were lucky because there had been a full moon, which usually makes catching prawns virtually impossible. Apparently, during the full moon prawns are easily seen by all kinds of hungry predators and so spend their time hidden under rocks, ledges and in groves of sea grass. There was a good catch of octopus, too, and as I know that Pete loves squid and octopus, I took some just for him.

We decided to look for more produce at the local Byron Bay Saturday Markets. It's a farmers'-direct market and most of their producers there are small time and organic, which means that the produce is sensational. We found exotic fruit, nuts, herbs, chutneys, sauces, wheat grass and eggs, and met Kay of Byron Sauces, from whom we got the most amazing lime dressing.

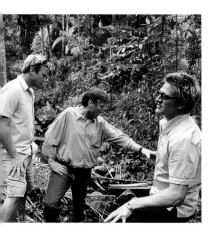

We also met Hugh, who farms free-range eggs. His family lives on one of the original Byron Bay cattle properties. He loves chooks and his mates call his place the 'Henhouse Hilton'. Better still, he's a surfer, so we made a date to catch up later that day. Hugh took us to some great out-of-the-way local breaks — when it comes to surfing, local knowledge is gold. The waves were wicked — small but great — and beautiful to surf.

I had decided to do a pork dish, as Dee's dad loves pork. Hugh suggested we take a drive to Bangalow and visit John the butcher. It's bloody beautiful once you get into the Byron Bay hinterland. It's a mix of rainforest and lush farmland. And it's green, every shade of green you can imagine.

Driving to Bangalow we were diverted by a small sign directing us to Brookfarm in St Helena. Here Pamela and Martin Brook grow macadamia nuts. They have 4500 trees snaking in row after row over the hills and into the valleys of their property. They don't just grow for nuts but for macadamia oil. The nuts are allowed to ripen on the tree and drop naturally to the ground. That's when they are harvested. Macadamias are native Australian rainforest trees and all the original plants that are now farmed around the world originally came from Australia.

Bangalow is a nice little town and the main street looks like it's out of a Ned Kelly movie set with its original heritage buildings dotting the main strip. At the butcher's shop we met the larger-than-life John Herane. John's is an old-fashioned butcher's shop with heaps of advice dispensed with every cut.

Last call was to the Zendvelds' coffee plantation. We were surprised to learn that coffee was grown in the Byron region — but it has been, since the 1880s. The Zendvelds have 20,000 trees under cultivation, which, by world standards is small, but they concentrate only on Arabica beans. Rebecca Zendveld showed us the trellised vines with beans ready for picking. They are bright red — it's no wonder they are called cherries. After picking, this red husk is removed because it's the bean, or seed, at the centre we're after. Even at this stage the bean doesn't look like what we know as coffee — it's a kind of beige colour and looks more like an overgrown lentil.

Then Rebecca took us into her dark domain — the roasting shed. She is the blender and roaster, and one of the few 'roast mistresses' in Australia. Roasting turns a simple bean into useable coffee. The roaster is to coffee as the winemaker and blender is to wine. When the roaster (the machine) is fired to the correct temperature, in go the raw beans. After that, there's a constant process of checking until the beans reach the colour Rebecca is looking for. The aroma in the shed is amazing. The beans are tumbled out of the roaster and onto a flat resting area where cool air is forced from below to stop them cooking. The coffee they make here is naturally low in caffeine. Apparently, low-quality soils produce high caffeine, as caffeine is nature's defence against pests. But here in the Byron highlands where volcanic soils are rich and pests few and far between, the coffee bushes don't need to make as much caffeine.

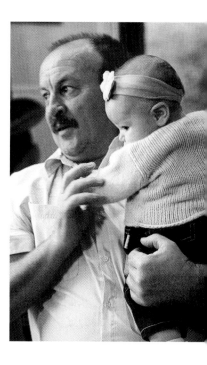

Once we'd found the pork, prawns and all the other accompaniments, Curtis and I headed to Peppers Resort in the rainforest where the family gathering had been arranged. A barbecue had been placed on the wide deck overlooking the natural rainforest valley. Curtis was a great help and we got stuck into preparing the food. Once the entire family had arrived, we fired up the barbie and got the show on the road. It was great fun with great food and great company. A fantastic way to end our short visit back in Oz.

Barbecued sweet corn with lime, chilli and Parmesan butter

The first time I tasted these flavours I was in New York at a little Cuban café on Prince Street, and thought wow! Now this recipe is a regular number on my barbecue menu at home. It's so simple to prepare, and great fun to eat.

SERVES 4

4 whole corn cobs, in their husks
100 g/3¹/₂ oz unsalted butter, softened
100 g/3¹/₂ oz Parmesan cheese, freshly grated
finely grated zest of 2 large limes
1–2 bird's-eye chillies, seeded and finely
    chopped
salt and freshly ground black pepper
1 lime, quartered

1 Place the corn cobs on a preheated hot grill and cook until golden brown, about 15 minutes, turning often. Peel off the husks when cool enough to handle.

2 While the corn is cooking, combine the butter, Parmesan, zest and chilli, and beat until smooth. Season with salt and pepper. Smear each cob with the butter and serve with a wedge of lime.

Ben O'Donoghue

Baby spinach and feta salad

This is your basic Greek salad, but better. It involves a little more work but, boy, the flavours — and it goes really well with Pete's octopus (page 238).

SERVES 4

1 large red onion, thinly sliced

2 Lebanese cucumbers (any cucumber
   will do), thinly sliced

1^1/$_2$ tablespoons caster sugar

1 tablespoon sea salt

2^1/$_2$ tablespoons white wine vinegar

3 tablespoons finely chopped dill

200 g/7 oz good quality feta cheese

4 loosley packed cups baby spinach,
   picked over

1 tablespoon aged balsamic vinegar

1 tablespoon extra virgin olive oil

55 g/2 oz pine nuts, toasted

1 Place the onion and cucumber in a glass bowl. Add the sugar, salt, white-wine vinegar and 1 tablespoon of dill. Leave for 30 minutes.

2 Break the feta into chunks and toss with the baby spinach and the remaining dill. Drain the onion and cucumber mixture and add to the feta. Add the balsamic vinegar and oil, and toss to coat. Sprinkle with the pine nuts to serve.

Ben O'Donoghue

Chinese-style combination soup

This soup is in the same family as the famous chicken and sweet corn and shark's fin soup. Basically, if you start off with a good base (stock) you can't go wrong. If you don't like any of the listed ingredients, then replace them with ones you do like. The soup is just so adaptable — if you prefer seafood, use fish stock and substitute the chicken and pork for crab and squid.

SERVES 6–8

2 L/3^1/$_2$ pints chicken stock
1 chicken breast fillet, weighing about
    225 g/8 oz
250 g/9 oz pork fillet
4 raw king prawns, peeled and deveined
1 carrot, thinly sliced
4 baby corn cobs, thinly sliced
100 g/3^1/$_2$ oz bamboo shoots, thinly sliced
4 tablespoons cornflour
4 tablespoons water
2 free-range eggs
1 bird's-eye chilli, finely chopped
8 spring onions, finely sliced
light soy sauce, to taste
fish sauce, to taste
sesame oil, to taste

1. Pour the stock into a large pot and bring to just below boiling. Add the chicken and pork, and poach for 2–3 minutes. Remove and cool for 10 minutes. Shred, then return to the stock.

2. Slice each prawn into six pieces. Add to the stock along with the carrot, corn and bamboo shoots. Bring to the boil. Blend the cornflour with the water, and slowly stir into the soup. Return to the boil, reduce heat, and simmer until thickened.

3. Crack the eggs into a small bowl and lightly beat with a fork. Remove the soup from the heat. While stirring in a circular motion, slowly add the eggs in a thin stream, creating egg flowers. Add the chilli and spring onion, and season to taste with light soy sauce, fish sauce and sesame oil.

Curtis Stone

Pete's octopus

In terms of food, Byron once meant avocados, macadamia nuts and magic mushrooms. Now it's all gourmet delicatessens, modern restaurants and growers' markets. Pete, my girlfriend's old man, loves octopus, so I thought that while I was in Byron Bay I had to dedicate a dish to him. He loves baby octopus, but I like the larger stuff; you can't have everything, mate. The best octopus to buy is the double-sucker variety; I don't know why, but they just cook up better. This recipe involves cooking the occy twice. It can be served with aioli, or any other dip you like, or with a Greek salad.

SERVES 4–6

1 large 2 kg/4^1/$_2$ lb double-sucker octopus
   (the suckers are usually side-by-side along
   the leg)
1 garlic clove, chopped
2 tablespoons chopped flat leaf parsley
1 tablespoon chopped thyme
1 dried chilli, crumbled
juice of 1 lemon
2 tablespoons olive oil

1. Preheat the oven to 130°C/250°F/Gas Mark 1, and place a wire rack over a baking tray. Cut the head off the octopus and discard. Rinse the body, remove the beak, then split the body in half to give two pieces with four tentacles each. Spread these on the wire rack and place the tray in the oven. Roast until the flesh is shrivelled and dry around the edges, but tender enough to push your fingers through, 2^1/$_2$–3 hours. Trim off the suckers and any overly dry bits.

2. Slice the tentacles into little fingers. Combine the garlic, parsley, thyme and chilli, and toss through the octopus. Add the lemon juice and oil and leave for 30 minutes. Place on a hot barbecue plate and grill until browned. Serve immediately.

Ben O'Donoghue

Salt and pepper prawns with an aromatic salad

The first time I ate salt and pepper squid, I was impressed with its simplicity. I went back to my kitchen and fiddled around with other seafood and found that prawns also work really well. Prawns cook very quickly, so try not to have them in the hot oil for more than a minute.

SERVES 4

12 raw king prawns
125 g/4^1/$_2$ oz cornflour
2 tablespoons sea salt
1 teaspoon freshly ground black pepper
large pinch dried chilli flakes
2 free-range eggs, lightly beaten
peanut (groundnut) oil,
    for deep-frying
1^1/$_2$ tablespoons olive oil
1 tablespoon lime juice
salt and freshly ground black pepper
6 cups loosely packed mixed salad and
    herb leaves (coriander, dill, basil,
    watercress, oak leaf lettuce, wild rocket)
3 punnets cherry tomatoes (red and yellow),
    quartered

1. Peel and devein the prawns, leaving the head and tail intact. Combine the cornflour with the salt, pepper and chilli flakes. Toss the prawns in the flour, dip in the egg mixture, then coat with the flour again.

2. Heat the peanut oil (5–6 cm/2–2^1/$_2$ in deep) in a pan. Fry the prawns, 3 or 4 at a time, until golden. Drain on paper towels. Mix the olive oil and lime juice together, and season to taste with salt and pepper. Toss through the salad leaves and tomato quarters. Pile one-quarter of the salad leaves in the centre of each of four serving plates and arrange the prawns around the salad.

Curtis Stone

King prawn, haloumi and pineapple skewers with lime, chilli and mint salsa

SERVES 4

12 long thick stalks of rosemary or
    bamboo skewers

Salsa
5 large red chillies, pricked with a fork
finely grated zest and juice of 1 lime
1 teaspoon sugar
5 tablespoons peanut (groundnut)
    or corn oil
leaves of ¼ bunch of mint, chopped
1 vine-ripened tomato, peeled, seeded and
    chopped
12 green king prawns, peeled and deveined
1 pineapple, peeled and chopped into
    equal-sized chunks
250 g/9 oz Haloumi cheese, chopped into
    equal-sized chunks

1. Strip the leaves from the rosemary stalks, keeping a tuft at the top. Soak stalks or skewers in cold water for 30 minutes to prevent them from burning on the barbecue.

2. To make the salsa, cook the chillies on a hot griddle plate or barbecue until charred. Place in a small bowl and cover with plastic wrap. When cool, remove the skin and seeds and tear the flesh into strips. Place in a clean bowl and toss with the lime zest and juice, sugar, oil, mint and tomatoes.

3. Thread a prawn, a piece of pineapple and a piece of cheese onto each skewer. Repeat once more, finishing each skewer with a prawn.

4. Grill on a hot griddle plate or barbecue until the prawns are cooked through and the pineapple and cheese are slightly charred, 5–8 minutes. Serve with a liberal drizzle of salsa.

Ben O'Donoghue

Caramelised spinach gnocchi and quattro formaggio

Gnocchi is one of those dishes that if it is done well, is fantastic. In this particular dish the gnocchi is pre-cooked and chilled, then just before serving, it is pan-fried. This makes the gnocchi crisp on the outside and nice and soft on the inside.

SERVES 4–6

500 g/1 lb 2 oz large floury potatoes, desiree are good
3 cups tightly packed spinach leaves
125 g/4¹/₂ oz pasta flour (00 Italian flour) plus 2–4 tablespoons extra
1 large free-range egg yolk
grated fresh nutmeg, to taste
salt and freshly ground black pepper

Sauce
250 mL/9 fl oz milk
150 mL/5¹/₂ fl oz pouring cream
45 g/1¹/₂ oz Taleggio cheese
45 g/1¹/₂ oz gorgonzola cheese
45 g/1¹/₂ oz mascarpone cheese
¹/₄ cup freshly grated Parmesan cheese
1 tablespoon finely chopped flat leaf parsley
salt and freshly ground black pepper
4 tightly packed cups spinach leaves
additional Parmesan cheese, shaved, to garnish

1 Preheat the oven to 180°C/350°F/Gas Mark 5. Place the potatoes on a baking tray and roast until tender, 1¹/₄–1¹/₂ hours, depending on size. Cool for 10 minutes. Halve and scoop out the flesh. While still warm, pass through a ricer or mouli. Do not use a food processor, as this will pulp the potatoes and draw out the starch. Cover and allow to cool.

2 Rinse the spinach and shake dry. Place in a large, hot saucepan and heat, tossing often, until wilted. Remove and chop finely. Transfer to a clean dry tea towel and squeeze out all the liquid.

3 Gently combine the potatoes, spinach, flour and egg yolk. Knead lightly for 15–20 seconds. You want a soft, lightly worked dough, so add extra flour only if the dough sticks to your hands. Season lightly with nutmeg, salt and pepper. Divide into three or four manageable portions and roll each into a log about the size of a breakfast sausage. Using a sharp knife, cut each log into 3 cm/1¹/₄ in lengths. Indent one side of the gnocchi with the tines of a fork. Place them in a single layer on a tray, and transfer to the refrigerator.

continued over...

Curtis Stone

4 Bring a large saucepan of salted water to the boil. Cook the gnocchi in batches until they float on the surface, 1–1^1/$_2$ minutes. Remove gnocchi and plunge into ice-cold water. Once cool, pat dry with kitchen paper. In a hot, non-stick frying pan, cook gnocchi until caramelised, or golden, on each side, about 1 minute.

5 To make the sauce, slowly bring the milk and cream to the boil. Add the four cheeses, reduce the heat and cook at a low simmer, stirring, until the cheeses melt. Purée, then pass through a sieve into a clean saucepan. Reheat, then add the parsley, and salt and pepper to taste.

6 Wilt the additional spinach in a hot pan, tossing frequently. Remove and chop finely. Squeeze out all liquid using a clean dry tea towel. Reheat in a little sauce.

7 To serve, divide the spinach evenly, placing it in the centre of the bowls. Spoon in equal quantities of the sauce, then divide the gnocchi among the bowls, arranging around the spinach. Garnish the spinach with shaved Parmesan.

Curtis Stone

Escalopes of pork with broad bean salad

This is another great summer recipe. Char-grilling pork gives it such a lovely flavour and with this lively salad the flavours are bright and light. I can just imagine the cool early evening breeze, with a nice chilled Sauvignon Blanc and the fresh flavours of this salad. Get your butcher to bash out four 2 cm/1 in thick cuts of pork loin which have a little fat left on the meat.

SERVES 4

Dry marinade

1 tablespoon finely chopped thyme

2 garlic cloves, finely chopped

finely grated zest of 2 lemons

$^1/_2$ teaspoon freshly ground black pepper

$^1/_2$ teaspoon lemon myrtle

4 pork escalopes, as above

Salad

1 kg/2 lb 4 oz unshelled fresh young
    broad beans*

150 g/5$^1/_2$ oz canned butter beans,
    drained

1 medium red onion, finely chopped

1$^1/_2$ cups loosely packed basil leaves,
    roughly torn

2 tablespoons chopped flat leaf parsley

Dressing

2$^1/_2$ tablespoons olive oil

juice of 2 lemons

salt and freshly ground black pepper

4 cups loosely packed wild rocket

1. To make the dry marinade, combine the thyme, garlic, zest, black pepper and lemon myrtle. Sprinkle over the pork and leave to stand for 15 minutes.

2. To make the salad, shell the broad beans. Combine with the butter beans, onion, basil and parsley.

3. To make the dressing, mix 2 tablespoons of the olive oil with half the lemon juice, and season to taste with salt and pepper. Pour half over the salad and toss lightly. Pour the remaining half over the rocket leaves and toss to coat.

4. Brush a preheated hot barbecue plate with oil and grill the pork, about 1 minute per side. Remove from the barbecue and squeeze with the remaining lemon juice.

5. Pile the bean salad in the centre of four serving plates. Top with an escalope of pork, then scatter the rocket over the top.

* Where fresh young broad beans are unavailable, use 500 g/1 lb 2 oz of shelled larger beans or frozen beans. Both will need to be blanched for 1 minute, then shelled.

Chocolate and espresso pudding

I do this dessert in my restaurant in London where it just flies out the door. Coffee is one of those flavours that goes well with chocolate. I like to use espresso coffee, but not everyone has an espresso machine so use a good quality instant coffee instead.

SERVES 6

Ice-cubes

55 g/2 oz milk chocolate, chopped

2¹⁄₂ tablespoons hot and very strong espresso coffee

Batter

250 g/9 oz dark chocolate (70 per cent cocoa solids), chopped

250 g/9 oz butter, cubed

8 free-range egg yolks

4 tablespoons rice flour

4 free-range egg whites

caster sugar, for dusting

icing sugar, for dusting

1 To make the ice-cubes, stir the chocolate and hot coffee together until melted and smooth. Divide between six ice-cube moulds and freeze until set, about 3 hours.

2 To make the batter, gently melt the chocolate and butter together in a heavy-based saucepan, stirring until smooth. Beat the egg yolks in a large bowl until light and fluffy, then fold through the chocolate mixture. Sift the rice flour into the bowl and stir to combine. Whisk the egg whites until soft peaks form and fold into the chocolate mixture. If necessary, the batter will keep for several hours.

3 Preheat the oven to 180°C/350°F/Gas Mark 5 and place a baking tray on the centre shelf. Butter six cappuccino cups or 150 mL/5 fl oz ovenproof cups, and dust with caster sugar. Spoon enough batter into the cups to fill by one-third. Place an ice-cube in the centre, then cover with the remaining batter. Transfer the cups to the baking tray.

continued over...

④ Place the baking tray in the oven and bake for 15–18 minutes. Turn the heat off and open the oven door. Leave the puddings to rest for 2 minutes.

⑤ To serve, gently run the tip of a knife around the edge of the puddings and turn out onto a plate. The outside should be the texture of a light sponge, with the centre runny. If you have difficulty in removing the pudding, just dust it with icing sugar and serve it in the cup.

Ben O'Donoghue

Chocolate fondant

The word fondant translates as melt. When you break into the pudding, the centre of it melts all over the plate. It's a bit like a self-saucing pudding — very indulgent, not something you eat every day, but if you decide to indulge, I promise you will be a repeat offender.

SERVES 4

cocoa, for dusting
200 g/7 oz dark chocolate, 70 per
    cent cocoa solids, chopped
200 g/7 oz butter
4 free-range eggs
4 free-range egg yolks
100 g/3$\frac{1}{2}$ oz sugar
55 g/2 oz flour

Sauce
250 mL/9 fl oz pouring cream
250 g/9 oz dark chocolate (70 per cent
    cocoa solids), chopped

vanilla ice-cream, to serve

1 Preheat the oven to 200°C/400°F/Gas Mark 7. Grease four dariole moulds (8 cm/3 in deep x 6 cm/2$\frac{1}{2}$ in wide) or four 1-cup ovenproof cups. Dust with cocoa, rolling each mould around to cover the walls well.

2 Melt the chocolate and butter over a low heat, stirring until smooth. Whisk the eggs, egg yolks and sugar until pale and doubled in volume, 3–4 minutes. Fold in the melted chocolate mixture. Add the flour, and whisk until smooth. Pour into the prepared moulds and bake until just set, 12–16 minutes. Rest for 3–4 minutes.

3 To make the sauce, bring the cream to just below boiling point in a heavy-based saucepan. Turn off the heat and add the chocolate. Stir constantly until melted and smooth.

4 To serve, run a sharp knife around the inside wall of each mould to loosen the fondant. Invert each mould over a serving plate and, holding the two together, give a sharp little shake to loosen. The fondant will slide out onto the plate. Serve with vanilla ice-cream and the chocolate sauce spooned over the top.

Curtis Stone

Pear and macadamia nut crumble

Macadamia nuts, like most nuts, have a high fat content. That is why they give a lovely richness to puddings and desserts, as well as being great in savoury dishes. Crumbles can be made out of a lot of different fruits, anything from pears to rhubarb to stone fruits.

SERVES 4–6

8 William pears, peeled, cored and
    quartered
100 g/3$^{1}/_{2}$ oz caster sugar
finely grated zest and juice of 1 orange
1 stick of cinnamon
1 vanilla pod, split in half lengthways

Crumble
280 g/10 oz plain flour
125 g/4$^{1}/_{2}$ oz caster sugar
100 g/3$^{1}/_{2}$ oz roasted and crushed
    macadamia nuts
125 g/4$^{1}/_{2}$ oz butter, softened

vanilla ice-cream, to serve

1 Place the pears in a medium saucepan with the sugar, zest and juice, cinnamon stick and vanilla bean. Cook, covered, over a moderate heat until the pears are tender, but not mushy, about 20 minutes, depending on the ripeness of the pears. Remove the cinnamon stick and vanilla pod.

2 Preheat the oven to 170°C/325°F/Gas Mark 4, and grease an ovenproof dish (30 cm/12 in x 15 cm/6 in and 8 cm/3$^{1}/_{4}$ in deep). Spoon the pears into the prepared dish.

3 For the crumble, combine the flour, sugar and macadamia nuts in a bowl. Add the butter and, using your fingers, rub it into the mixture until evenly distributed. Scatter over the pears and transfer the dish to the oven. Bake for 15–20 minutes, or until golden brown on top. Serve warm, with vanilla ice-cream.

Curtis Stone

Index

Conversion chart

75 mL	2½ fl oz
100 mL	3½ fl oz
125 mL	4½ fl oz
150 mL	5½ fl oz
200 mL	7 fl oz
250 mL	9 fl oz
300 mL	10½ fl oz
450 mL	¾ pt
500 mL	18 fl oz
600 mL	1 pt
800 mL	1½ pt
1 L	1¾ pt
1.2 L	2 pt
1.5 L	2⅔ pt
2 L	3½ pt
2.5 L	4½ pt
4 L	7 pt

15 g	½ oz
30 g	1 oz
55 g	2 oz
75 g	2¾ oz
100 g	3½ oz
125 g	4½ oz
150 g	5½ oz
200 g	7 oz
225 g	8 oz
250 g	9 oz
300 g	11 oz
350 g	12 oz
400 g	14 oz
450 g	1 lb
500 g	1 lb 2 oz
700 g	1½ lb
900 g	2 lb
1 kg	2 lb 4 oz
1.2 kg	¾ lb
1.4 kg	3 lb
1.5 kg	3 lb 5 oz
2 kg	4½ lb
5 kg	11 lb